PublicServicePrep Comprehensive Guide to Canadian Military, Border Services, Corrections and Security Exams

COMPREHNSIVE GUIDE TO CANADIAN MILITARY, BORDER SERVICES, CORRECTIONS AND SECURITY EXAMS, published by:

PublicServicePrep
http://www.publicserviceprep.com
info@publicserviceprep.com

Authors:
Deland Jessop, Kalpesh Rathod, and Adam Cooper.

ISBN 978-0-9866687-0-8

Printed and bound in Canada

Table of Contents

Introduction – Public Service

Welcome to PublicServicePrep. The application process for government jobs can be very competitive. We understand the situation you're in and the challenges that lie ahead for you. This study guide was developed to help you prepare for the public service exams used by government bodies across Canada.

By purchasing this guide, you have taken the most important step - you have moved from thinking about preparation to taking action. Your dedication to preparing for your entrance exams demonstrates that you are the motivated person government services want to hire.

If you are looking for more practice tests and further preparation materials, visit our website at WWW.PUBLICSERVICEPREP.COM. We offer a special discount of 25% for those who have purchased this guide. When signing up online input the following code in the referral code section to get the discount (note the code is case sensitive):

ppdc712

Please do not hesitate to contact us if you have any questions, concerns or comments about this book, our website, or the application and testing process. We will be happy to do anything we can to assist you.

Email: info@publicserviceprep.com
URL: http://www.publicserviceprep.com

Introduction – Security / Private Investigation

Welcome to PolicePrep. Our online Security Guard / Private Investigation test prep course is designed to help you ace the new certification test required by the Ontario Ministry of Community Safety and Correctional Services, as well as prepare for other licencing and testing performed throughout the country.

If you are looking for more practice tests and further preparation materials, visit our website at WWW.POLICEPREP.COM. We offer a special discount of 25% for those who have purchased this guide. When signing up online input the following code in the referral code section to get the discount (note the code is case sensitive):

secure11

Please do not hesitate to contact us if you have any questions, concerns or comments about this book, our website, or the application and testing process. We will be happy to do anything we can to assist you.

Email: info@policeprep.com
URL: http://www.policeprep.com

ATTENTION STUDENTS

With the purchase of this book you receive a life-time online membership to PolicePrep.
Online Access Code:

YCK8-RQ2J-DAAC

Register your account at: **www.PolicePrep.com/registration**
Enter the <u>above</u> Online Access Code when prompted.
(Do <u>NOT</u> use the "ppdc1320" referral code!)

Preparation Material

Resume Building

A resume is a tool you can use to demonstrate your fit for the job-specific requirements of a career. Few people have received instruction on building a resume, or had much experience writing them. They don't understand what should or should not be included to present themselves in the best manner they can.

Resume building does not start at the writing stage. If you are serious about applying for a government position, you should have a long list of volunteer experience, academic achievements, languages, computer skills and other highlights to place on your resume. If you don't, begin today. Many organizations, including food banks, charity organizations and Children's Aid Societies are desperate for volunteer help. Languages, especially French are important for government agencies, as are computer skills and any other life skills.

The main purpose of your resume is to frame your experiences, skills and knowledge in a manner relevant to the position to which you are applying. You have to not only demonstrate what you've done, but also show that you have done it well. It is crucial to present information clearly and concisely so the person reviewing your resume can quickly find what they require. Three principles should be followed:

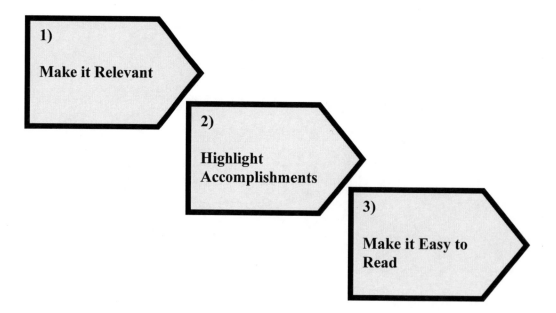

1) Make it Relevant

2) Highlight Accomplishments

3) Make it Easy to Read

Principle One: Make it Relevant

Government agencies want to fill positions with people who fit their needs. It is important to determine what competencies are required for the job. Below is a sample list of competencies that may be useful for many government jobs.

Analytical Thinking	The ability to analyze situations and events in a logical way, and to organize the parts of a problem systematically.
Self – Confidence	A belief in your capabilities and recognition of personal limitations.
Communication	You must have the skills to effectively communicate using listening skills and verbal and written communications skills.
Flexibility / Valuing Diversity	With government jobs, you will have to work with a wide cross-section of the community with diverse backgrounds, cultures and socio-economic circumstances. You must have the ability to adapt your approach to each situation.
Self - Control	You must establish that you can control your emotions and actions when provoked.
Relationship Building	Developing contacts and relationships both within and outside your area of employment is extremely valuable.
Achievement Orientation	You must demonstrate a desire for continuous improvement in service and accomplishments.
Information Seeking	The ability to seek out and consider information from various sources before making decisions.
Assertiveness	The capacity to use authority confidently and to set and enforce rules appropriately.
Initiative	Demonstrated proficiency to be self-motivated and self-directed in identifying and addressing important issues.
Cooperation	Willing to act with others by seeking their input, encouraging their participation and sharing information.

Negotiation / Facilitation	The ability to influence and persuade others by anticipating and addressing their interests and perspectives.
Work Organization	The ability to develop and maintain systems for organizing information and activities.
Community Service Orientation	Proven commitment to helping or serving others.
Commitment to Learning	Demonstrated pattern of activities that contribute to personal and professional growth.
Organization Awareness	A capacity for understanding the dynamics of organizations, including the formal and informal cultures and decision-making processes.
Developing Others	Commitment to helping others improve their skills.

Many people squeeze everything into a resume hoping that something will click. Any material on your resume that does not exhibit traits from the list of core competencies the agency is looking for is a waste of space.

Do not include every employer on your resume unless you are specifically asked to provide that information. Many government agencies require an employment history application. Pick out the most relevant positions you have had and focus on demonstrating the qualities. Any additional information such as Activities, Volunteer Experience, Education, or Special Skills should also demonstrate your competencies.

Principle Two: Highlight Accomplishments

Accomplishment statements should give your potential employer an indication of how well you performed. It should reveal not only what you did, but also how well you did it. Each statement should include the following:

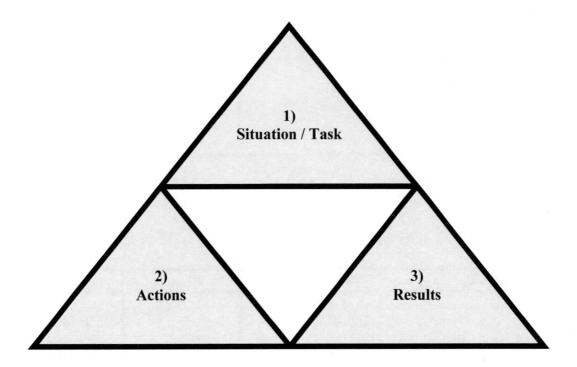

Each accomplishment should describe skills relevant to the job you're applying for. Practice writing these statements. Typically, accomplishment statements fall under the Work Experience, Volunteer Experience, or Education sections of your resume.

Example Action Statements

1) Day Camp Counsellor

Core Competency	Situation / Task	Action	Result
Developing Others, Cooperation, Assertiveness, Community Service, Communication.	Field trips as a day camp counsellor.	Instruction and supervision.	Ensured safety of 60 children with fellow counsellors.

"Supervised and instructed 60 young children on field trips ensuring their safety and enjoyment with a team of fellow counsellors."

2) Retail / Grocery

Core Competency	Situation / Task	Action	Result
Work Organization, Communication, Negotiation / Facilitation	Controlling Inventory.	Organized units and placed orders (quantified)	Diverse customer's needs anticipated and satisfied.

"Organized shelving units and placed orders in excess of $20,000 ensuring diverse customer needs were anticipated and satisfied."

3) Post-Secondary Education

Core Competency	Situation / Task	Action	Result
Initiative, Achievement Orientation, Analytical Thinking, Commitment to Learning, Communication	Attending post-secondary education.	Studied sociology (or any other major)	Graduated with a strong standing, developing a core set of skills.

"Developed analytical, presentation, computer and XXXX skills, studying sociology and graduating with a 75% average."

4) Volunteer Work

Core Competency	Situation / Task	Action	Result
Initiative, Communication, Cooperation, Work Organization, Developing Others, Self-Confidence, Flexibility / Valuing Diversity, Negotiation / Facilitation, Community Service Orientation	Food drive at work.	Organized and implemented.	Raised $2,000 for needy people in the community.

"Organized and implemented a Food Drive with a team of volunteers, effectively raising $2,000 for needy people in the community."

Action Verbs to be used for your Accomplishment Statements

Accelerated	Displayed	Negotiated	Saved
Accumulated	Documented	Ordered	Scheduled
Accomplished	Effected	Organized	Selected
Acquired	Enforced	Performed	Separated
Analyzed	Engineered	Perpetuated	Served
Applied	Evaluated	Planned	Set
Arranged	Facilitated	Prepared	Shared
Assessed	Filed	Prescribed	Showed
Authorized	Financed	Presented	Solved
Approved	Founded	Problem-solved	Strengthened
Began	Generated	Processed	Succeeded
Bought	Hired	Produced	Supplied
Budgeted	Identified	Promoted	Taught
Coached	Implemented	Provided	Team-built
Collected	Invented	Questioned	Trained
Combined	Launched	Raised	Translated
Communicated	Learned	Read	Tutored
Conducted	Made	Realized	Uncovered
Convinced	Maintained	Reorganized	Unified
Coordinated	Managed	Repaired	Utilized
Developed	Marketed	Researched	Vitalized
Directed	Minimized	Revised	Won
Discovered	Monitored	Risked	Wrote

Principle 3 - Make it Easy to Read

Recruiters may look at thousands of resumes each year. They do not necessarily spend a lot of time on each one. This means your resume has only a few minutes to prove that you are a good fit for the job. The information presented has to be immediately pertinent and easy to read. Key things you should be mindful of when finishing up your resume are:

- use high quality bond paper
- incorporate as much white space as possible so the reader is not overwhelmed
- highlight only key words or positions to attract attention
- use bullet points rather than paragraphs
- keep font sizes between 10 and 12 pt

Language and grammar are very important to a resume and the following should be observed:

- make every word count
- use short, simple and concrete words that are easily understood
- use strong nouns and vital verbs to add action, power and interest
- avoid personal pronouns
- spell check the document and always have someone proof read the material
- double check the meaning of easily confused words, i.e.:

  affect (influence) vs. effect (result)
  personal (private) vs. personnel (staff)
  elicit (draw forth) vs. illicit (unlawful)
  discreet (showing good judgement) vs. discrete (distinct or separate)
  allude (indirect reference) vs. elude (to evade)

A few rules-of-thumb

- months do not need to be included in dates when the length of employment is greater than six months
- part-time and full-time descriptors are generally not included
- do not include names of supervisors
- check with the government service to which you are applying to about disclosing full employment history

Review the copy of the sample resume below.

Resume Components

Name	Address Telephone Number E-mail

Education

Educational Institution Location Degree	Date
Educational Institution Location Degree	Date

Work Experience

Company, Geographic Location Position title - Descriptive Statement if needed - Relevant Accomplishment Statement - Relevant Accomplishment Statement	Date
Company, Geographic Location Position title - Descriptive Statement if needed - Relevant Accomplishment Statement - Relevant Accomplishment Statement	Date
Company, Geographic Location Position title - Descriptive Statement if needed - Relevant Accomplishment Statement - Relevant Accomplishment Statement	Date

Examples of Optional Section Headings

- Professional Development	- Awards
- Computer Skills	- Summary of Qualifications
- Languages	- Functional Skills
- Activities and Interests	- Publications
- Volunteer Experience	- Academic Achievements

Jane / John Doe (EXAMPLE)
2 / 2 Wellington Crescent, Winnipeg, Manitoba   Phone: (204) 555-1212
johndoe@xxx.ca

Education

CITY COLLEGE, Winnipeg, Manitoba   (20xx – 20xx)
Police Investigations Diploma
- Elected Class President and managed a budget of $5,000 and a team of 15 volunteers to deliver class social activities and educational assistance programs.

MAIN STREET COLLEGIATE, Brandon, Manitoba   (20xx – 20xx)
OSSD, OAC Certificate, Honour Roll, Senior English Award

Professional Experience

You Name It Security, Vancouver, British Columbia   (20xx-present)
Security Guard
- Investigated and handled property disturbances arising from a variety of situations, and resulting in reports, cautions or arrests.
- Organized and implemented a neighbourhood watch program for clients taking a proactive role to reduce instances of break and enters in a residential complex.

Toronto Parks Department, Toronto, Ontario   (20xx – 20xx)
Assistant Activity Implementer
- Scheduled and implemented a variety of after school activities for 50 – 60 children with fellow co-workers.
- Used a needs-based approach to assist children from diverse cultural backgrounds with a variety of problems such as schoolwork, bullying and loneliness.

Volunteer
- Thanksgiving Food Drive - annually delivering food to needy people throughout the community
- Children's Aid Society – Special Buddy Program   (20xx – 20xx)
- City College Orientation Leader   (20xx)

Interests
- Shodan Black Belt in Jiu Jitsu, running, weight training, snowboarding, rock climbing, white water rafting, sport parachuting, water skiing and SCUBA diving.
- Piano – Royal Conservatory Grade 5. Guitar - Introductory lessons.

Computer Skills
- Excel, WordPerfect, PowerPoint
- Internet development, Outlook

The Interview

It is important to recognize that government agencies are looking for the best people for the job and will not try to consciously confuse you.

At this stage it is your interpersonal and communication skills that will help you land a job. The interviewer is looking for someone who is competent, likeable and who fits in with the organization's culture, goals, beliefs and values.

What Interviewers Tend to Look For

Friendly Personality

With many government jobs, you spend a great deal of time with co-workers. Every interviewer will ask themselves whether or not they would enjoy working with you. You must prove that you are likeable enough to do this.

Organizational Fit

Many organizations may have a very particular culture and it is important for interviewers to ensure that job applicants will fit that culture. Suitability may include the willingness to work shift work and overtime if required, give up days off if required, or an ability to function well as a member of a team.

It is important not to pretend to be something you're not. If you feel you wouldn't fit in with an organization's culture, then it is probably best for both you and the organization that you seek another career. It is important to ask these questions of yourself. Once in the interview stage, you should be confident that you would fit in with the culture.

Capable and Professional

Government organizations want competent personnel. You must demonstrate that you are capable of handling responsibility and that you can perform the required tasks. It would be prudent to review any core competencies required for the job to which you are applying.

Handling Pre-Interview Stress

Feeling nervous before an interview is perfectly normal. Politicians, entertainers and media personalities feel nervous prior to performances as well. The best way to handle the stress is to be well prepared. Once again, interviewers are not trying to trick you. They want you to succeed; it makes their job easier. Some things you should do before the interview include:

- Get a good night's sleep (this goes without saying, but bears repeating).
- Practice interviewing with friends, using the behavioural questions below.
- Wear professional clothing (suits or business dress).

You should bring all of the documents that are requested from you (transcripts, copy of your resume, portfolio) to the interview along with a pad of paper, a pen, a list of references and a list of questions you may have. Interviewers are often impressed if you have intelligent and researched questions about the job.

How to Influence the Hiring Decision

Understand the Organization – Local Focus Interviews

It is important to have at least a rudimentary understanding of the organization to which you are applying. This information is available on most websites, or at employment offices where you are applying. Some information you should know would include:

- Rough size of the organization or group with which you will work. (example: Canadian Forces have 62,000 regular members, 25,000 reserve members and 4,000 Canadian Rangers)
- Name of the managers or politicians in charge of departments. (example: Minister of Finance.)
- The challenge that all government services are facing (asked to do more with less, budget constraints, intense scrutiny, etc.)

Before any interview, make a habit of reading the newspaper and checking the internet for news about the department you are applying to, so that you are aware of the local issues and concerns of the area.

Understand the Job

You have to understand the job to which you are applying. Gather as much information about the job as you can, including typical tasks, where your office would be, career paths, etc. To prove that you understand the job, make sure that you include the less glamorous duties that it might entail (filing reports, answering phones, dealing with the public, etc.).

Understand Yourself

When you are involved with an interview, it is extremely important to be very familiar with your resume and past situations in your life. You will more than likely encounter questions about your past acts, goals and emotions. The list below includes a number of questions you should be familiar with prior to any interview.

- How have you prepared for this position and what are your qualifications?
- What are your greatest strengths and weaknesses?
- How do you get along with co-workers?
- Why are you pursuing a career with this department?
- What motivates you to perform well?
- What are your three greatest accomplishments in life?
- How would you work under pressure?

First Impressions

First impressions are extremely important. Many judgements are made about a person within the first 30 seconds of an encounter (fairly or unfairly). It is your job to impress the interviewer(s). Three basic steps you can take to ensure that you make a great first impression are:

Look Professional	**Be Confident**	**Break the Ice**
Interviewers want to see an applicant who respects them enough to wear the appropriate attire.	Greet the interviewer (s) with a smile, a firm handshake, a relaxed manner and a friendly "Hello".	Engage in small talk. It can be about anything, (weather, traffic, etc). It doesn't have to be profound. It's meant to put both parties at ease.

Communication and Interpersonal Effectiveness

The interview process is a situation that tests your communication skills. You should be aware of the following:

Eye Contact	Maintain eye contact with the person you are addressing. This means looking at the person who is speaking to you. In interviews with more than one interviewer spend an equal amount of time on each person.
Body Language	Be aware of your position in your seat and your breathing pattern. Attempt to relax by taking steady breaths. Make sure you sit up straight in an interview. This will exhibit self-confidence and professionalism.
Gestures and Speech	Be aware of any gestures you use. Nod and maintain eye contact to indicate that you understand interview questions. Smile when appropriate, and be vocally expressive by alternating your tone where necessary. Be natural and avoid filler words such as "umm" and "like".

During the Interview

Make an effort to read the interviewers. Ask yourself whether they appear to be straining to follow you, if you are talking too fast (breathe more deeply), or too softly (speak louder). If they are writing frantically, that is usually a good sign, but make occasional pauses so that they can keep up. If you do not understand a question, ask them to repeat or clarify it. If you do not know the answer to one of their questions, admit it. Do not lie during the interview.

Prepare Stories Prior to the Interview

Interviewers may have some questions regarding your resume, or your past experiences. Make sure you are familiar with the content in your resume, and any tasks that you mention in it.

Many government agencies will use a behavioural-based interview method. This means that they will ask you questions about yourself and will ask you to describe events that have actually occurred in your past (usually the last two years). Some examples of questions you should be prepared to answer include:

Give an example in your life when you:

- were involved in a stressful situation and how you dealt with it.
- were extremely angry and how you dealt with it.
- had to take the role of a leader, and how was the situation resolved.
- had to work as part of a team and explain what happened.
- had to resolve a conflict with other parties and how did you handled it.
- were up against an important deadline and how you handled the work.
- had a conflict with a supervisor and how you handled it.

There are many other behavioural questions, but these are some of the most common examples.

How to Answer Behavioural Based Questions

Each behavioural question is a story about your past. Make sure that the story you tell is relevant, clear, and even interesting (interviewers are only human). Each story should have:

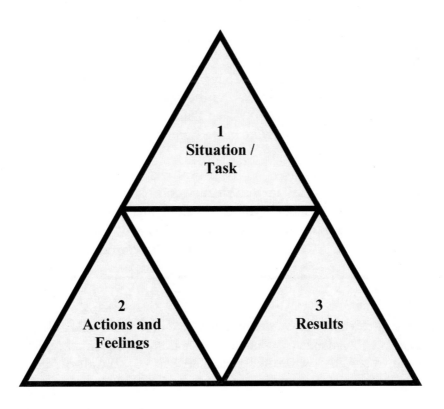

Step One - Understand the Question

This is vital. If you do not understand the question or what the interviewer is asking for, ask them to repeat it or explain it. There is no point giving a very effective answer to the wrong question. For example: one interviewee, asked about Ethnicity, spoke a great deal about Ethics during an interview. The interviewers probably thought he was an idiot, but he was probably just nervous and didn't hear the question properly.

Step Two - Brief Synopsis

Let the interviewers know what you plan to talk about with a brief outline of the situation, with little detail. This will give you some time to organize your thoughts and the interviewers will understand where you are going. This should take no longer than a couple of sentences.

> **Example:**
>
> "I am going to tell you about a conflict I had with my boss while I was working as a personal trainer. It involved a situation where I was told to bill a client at a rate I didn't feel was justified. We dealt with it away from the customer and resolved it in a manner that satisfied myself, the manager, and the client."

Step Three - Full Story

A retelling of the story will demonstrate to the interviewers your competencies in dealing with the situation and your communication capabilities. Interviewers want a clear story, preferably in a chronological sequence. They are most concerned with your feelings during the situation, the actions you took, and the result of your actions. Always finish the story with the results of your actions. Keep these points in mind both while you are preparing for the interview, and when you are participating in it:

- Answer the question asked.
- Pause and think – don't rush in with an answer.
- Pay attention to the pronouns you are using. Interviewers want to know what "YOU" did. Use the pronoun "I" for your actions and "Us" for team actions. **DO NOT ALWAYS USE "WE".** You will fail the interview.

> **Bad Example:**
>
> "We formed a team to solve the problem. We brainstormed an idea to solve the problem. We then decided on a course of action and began to implement it. We handled task "A" while others handled task "B". We all had individual assignments."

> **Good Example**:
>
> "I formed a team to solve a problem. We brainstormed an idea to solve the problem. I then had to decide the course of action and we began to implement. My friend John and I were responsible for task "A" while another group handled task "B". My particular assignment was to do "X".

- Ensure you effectively explain the situation, your feelings, your actions and the result.
- If necessary take pauses to collect your thoughts. There is no need to be constantly talking.
- Relax and enjoy telling the story. You should know it well, as you actually did it.
- Give focused and fluid answers.
- Avoid run-on answers.
- Give support for claims that are made, if possible.
- Show evidence of preparation work.

Other Interviewing Methods

You should be aware that you could be asked technical or "what if" questions or questions about your past. Some agencies may ask:

- What would you do if you caught a co-worker stealing?
- Have you ever smoked marijuana?
- Have you ever stolen anything?
- Have you ever committed an illegal act?

It is important to give these questions careful consideration and answer honestly. If you tried smoking marijuana when you were in high school, admit it and tell the interviewer why you didn't continue to use it. For example, you found it hurt the academic performance of your friends, or something along those lines.

"What if" questions are intended to challenge you, to see if you are the type of person who will immediately back down. This is not a trait agencies are looking for. Once you have made up your mind on an issue, stand by it. Interviewers may challenge you but this is part of the process. Just ensure that you give careful thought to the question to avoid defending a weak position. It is acceptable to credit the other opinion, but do not change your decision.

On top of these questions, you may receive some technical questions when applying to specific positions

Completing the Interview

Just like the first impression, it is important to give a positive impression during the last few moments of an interview. If you have any questions for the interviewers, the end of the interview is when they should be asked. It is acceptable to have prepared questions written down. As you are leaving the room, smile at the interviewer(s) individually, walk up to each one, look into their eyes, shake their hands and personally thank them for their time.

General Suggestions

Preparation Prior to Testing

Check out the websites and contact the government agency to ensure that you are familiar with the testing procedures and the content of the exams. It is important to get as much information as possible from the department to which you are applying.

Practice on numerous tests to ensure that you are familiar with the content of the testing material.

Before Testing

Get enough sleep before the tests and enough food and water even if you are nervous prior to entering the test. Try to remain relaxed and comfortable. Wear clothing that is professional, but also comfortable to work in. Arrive early and ready to begin.

During the Test

Don't waste time on a question you are unable to answer; take a guess and move onto the next question. Make a note of answers you are not certain of, and review them if you have time after answering the remaining questions.

Pay attention to the answer sheet and the question number. Many applicants have failed as the result of an error on the scoring card. Every time you respond to a question, look at the answer card carefully and make sure that the number you are answering on the card matches the number of the question.

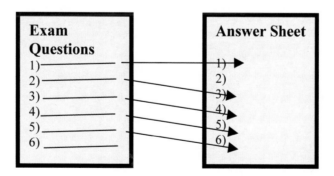

In the above example, even if the applicant answered the questions correctly, the applicant would only get one out of the six questions right because of the errors on the scoring card. Keep this in mind when taking the test. You will not be able to correct or explain yourself if you make a mistake on the score card because they are computer scored. This mistake is more common if you if you decide to skip a particular question. In the event that you decide to skip questions, a tactic to avoid making an order error is to cross off the question you skipped on the answer card.

Teaching Material Math

Addition

$$7 + 5 = 12$$

(vertical:)
```
    7
+   5
   12
```

The above two equations have the same value and are very straightforward. It is important to know that the order of numbers does not make a difference in addition (or multiplication). For example:

```
    6                      3
+   3        same      +   6
    9                      9
```

$$243 + 716 = 959$$
same
$$716 + 243 = 959$$

Some complications arise when larger numbers are used and you need to carry numbers.

Note: When you see a math problem laid out horizontally, as in the box immediately above, rearrange the numbers so that they are vertical (on top of each other) to make the addition easier to do.

Example:

```
  3 5 1
  6 9 9
+ 4 5 7
```

(A)
```
  3 5 1
  6 9 9
+ 4 5 7
     17
```

(B)
```
    1
  3 5 1
  6 9 9
+ 4 5 7
   20 7
```

(C)
```
    2
  3 5 1
  6 9 9
+ 4 5 7
 15 0 7
```

(A)
Start by adding up the numbers in the right most column. The result is 17. The seven remains but the one is carried over to be added to the next column of numbers.

(B)
The same rules apply to the sum 20 in the second column. The 0 remains in the second row, while the 2 is carried over to the column to the left to be added.

(C)
The final column is then added and the answer is recorded.

₃traction

$$\begin{array}{r} 8 \\ -\ \ 3 \\ \hline 5 \end{array}$$ $8 - 3 = 5$

The above two equations have the same value and are very straightforward. It is important to know that the order of numbers is significant in subtraction (and division). Different ordering will result in different answers. For example:

$$\begin{array}{r} 18 \\ -\ \ 3 \\ \hline 15 \end{array}$$ different $$\begin{array}{r} 3 \\ -\ 18 \\ \hline -\ 15 \end{array}$$

$$712 - 245 = \ \ 467$$
different
$$245 - 712 = -467$$

Some complications arise when larger numbers are used and you need to carry numbers.

Example:

$$\begin{array}{r} 7\ 4\ 3 \\ -\ 5\ 8\ 9 \\ \hline \end{array}$$

(A)

$$\begin{array}{r} 3 \\ 7\ \cancel{4}\ {}_13 \\ -\ 5\ 8\ 9 \\ \hline 4 \end{array}$$

(B)

$$\begin{array}{r} 6\ \ \ 13 \\ \cancel{7}\ \cancel{4}\ 3 \\ -\ 5\ 8\ 9 \\ \hline 1\ 5\ 4 \end{array}$$

(A)

The first task is to subtract the right most column. Because 9 is larger than 3, a unit has to be borrowed from the column to the left. The 4 in the middle column is reduced to 3, and the one is added to the right column, making the first row $13 - 9 = 4$.

(B)

The second task is to subtract the second column. The same process is repeated. Borrow a 1 from the left column to allow the subtraction. The top number in the left column becomes 6, while the top number in the centre column becomes 13. $13 - 8 = 5$. The left column would then be subtracted. $6 - 5 = 1$.

Note: If subtracting more than 2 numbers, you cannot stack the numbers as you would in addition. Instead, work from the first subtraction to the last, two numbers at a time.

Multiplication

$$
\begin{array}{r}
8 \\
\times \quad 6 \\
\hline
48
\end{array}
$$

$8 \times 6 = 48$

The above two equations have the same value and are very straightforward. It is important to know that the order of numbers makes no difference in multiplication (or addition). For example:

$$
\begin{array}{r}
7 \\
\times \quad 8 \\
\hline
56
\end{array}
$$

same

$$
\begin{array}{r}
8 \\
\times \quad 7 \\
\hline
56
\end{array}
$$

$245 \times 233 = 57{,}085$

same

$233 \times 245 = 57{,}085$

Multiplication, simply put, is adding groups of numbers. For instance, in the above example, the number 8 is being added six times.

$8 \times 6 = 48$	$7 \times 7 = 49$
$8 + 8 + 8 + 8 + 8 + 8 = 48$	$7 + 7 + 7 + 7 + 7 + 7 + 7 = 49$
$9 \times 5 = 45$	$6 \times 3 = 18$
$9 + 9 + 9 + 9 + 9 = 45$	$6 + 6 + 6 = 18$

It will be difficult to pass an exam if you have to calculate all simple multiplication in this manner. You should memorize the basic multiplication tables for 1 through 12. Review the multiplication table in this book.

Some complications arise when larger numbers are used and you need to carry numbers.

Example:

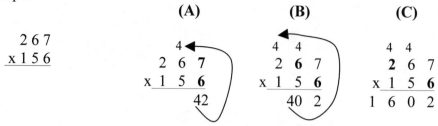

```
      2 6 7
    x 1 5 6
```

(A)

Begin by multiplying out the right row. The 2 is recorded in the right column and the 4 is transferred to the middle column and recorded as above.

(B)

The second step is to multiply the 6 in the middle column. 6 x 6 = 36. The 4 that was carried over from step A has to be added to the 36. The result is 40 and the 0 is recorded in the middle column. The four is then carried forward to left column as in step A.

(C)

The 6 then has to be multiplied to the left digit on the top number. 6 x 2 = 12. The four that was carried over from step B is added to the 12. The result is 16 and recorded as shown.

(D)   **(E)**   **(F)**

```
        3              3   3            3   3
      2 6 7          2 6 7            2 6 7
    x   1 5 6      x   1 5 6        x   1 5 6
    1 6 0 2        1 6 0 2          1 6 0 2
        35 0          33 5 0      1 3 3 5 0
```

(D-F)

The next steps are to multiply the second digit in the bottom row (the 5) to each of the top digits. The 5 is multiplied to the 7, the 6 and the 2. The process is the same as steps A - C. If the number is 10 or larger the number is carried over, as above, and added to the next multiplication.

It is important to remember that the next multiplication set has to be recorded on the line below and lined up starting in the next column. Place a zero in the right column to ensure the digits line up properly

	(G)			**(H)**			**(I)**	

```
        (G)                    (H)                    (I)

        2  6  7                2  6  7                2  6  7
    x   1  5  6            x   1  5  6            x   1  5  6
    1   6  0  2            1   6  0  2            1   6  0  2
 1  3  3  5  0         1  3  3  5  0         1  3  3  5  0
       7  0  0            6  7  0  0         2  6  7  0  0
```

The next steps are to multiply the left digit in the bottom number by each of the digits in the top number. The same process is used as outlined above if numbers have to be carried over.

Lining up of the digits is also necessary at this stage. Because you are multiplying from the hundreds column (the left most) you begin recording the answer in the hundreds column. Follow the same procedure as outlined above. Fill in the first two columns with zeros.

```
           2  6  7
       x   1  5  6
       1   6  0  2
    1  3  3  5  0
 +  2  6  7  0  0
    4  1  6  5  2
```

The final step is to add up the three numbers that were multiplied out. Treat the addition of these three numbers exactly as you would a regular addition problem. If you failed to line the numbers up properly, you will wind up with an incorrect answer. 41,652 is the final answer.

Note: Because complex multiplication questions (like the one above) involve addition, make sure you have a firm grasp of the addition section before trying to tackle multiplication.

Things to Watch For

Watch out for a multiplication question where the first digit in the bottom number is a zero, or where there are zeros in the equation. You still have to properly line up the digits. Note the highlighted zeros.

```
      3 4 5
  x       5 0
  1 7 2 5 0
```

Remember that zero multiplied by any other number is zero. In this situation you begin multiplying with the 10's column (the 5). Because you are multiplying from the 10's column, you begin recording your answer there. Place a zero in the first column.

```
        3
      6 0 9
  x         4
    2 4 3 6
```

When the four is multiplied to the 0, the result is 0. The number, which is carried over from multiplying 9 x 4 has to be added to 0, which results in the highlighted answer - 3.

```
        4 5 2
    x   3 0 9
        4 0 6 8
  + 1 3 5 6 0 0
    1 3 9 6 6 8
```

In this situation there is no need to multiply the bottom ten's digit out, as the result will equal 0. You must, however, properly line up the numbers. Because the 3 is in the hundred's column, you must begin recording your answer in the hundred's column. That is why there are two highlighted zeros.

Multiplication Tables

	1	2	3	4	5	6	7	8	9	10	11	12
1	1	2	3	4	5	6	7	8	9	10	11	12
2	2	4	6	8	10	12	14	16	18	20	22	24
3	3	6	9	12	15	18	21	24	27	30	33	36
4	4	8	12	16	20	24	28	32	36	40	44	48
5	5	10	15	20	25	30	35	40	45	50	55	60
6	6	12	18	24	30	36	42	48	54	60	66	72
7	7	14	21	28	35	42	49	56	63	70	77	84
8	8	16	24	32	40	48	56	64	72	80	88	96
9	9	18	27	36	45	54	63	72	81	90	99	108
10	10	20	30	40	50	60	70	80	90	100	110	120
11	11	22	33	44	55	66	77	88	99	110	121	132
12	12	24	36	48	60	72	84	96	108	120	132	144

Use of the Table

To use this table, take a number along the top axis and multiply it by a number along the side axis. Where they intersect is the answer to the equation. An example of this is 7 x 3. If you find 7 on the side axis and follow the row until you reach the 3 column on the top axis, you will find the answer – 21.

Look for simple patterns to assist your memorization efforts. For example:

Whenever 10 is multiplied to another number, just add a zero.

    10 x 3 = 30   10 x 7 = 70
    10 x 10 = 100   10 x 12 = 120

Whenever 11 is multiplied by a number less than 9, just double the digit 11 is multiplied by.

    11 x 3 = 33   11 x 5 = 55
    11 x 7 = 77   11 x 9 = 99

One multiplied by any other number is always equal to that number.

    1 x 1 = 1   1 x 4 = 4
    1 x 8 = 8   1 x 12 = 12

Zero multiplied to any number is always zero.

    0 x 10 = 0   0 x 3 = 0

Nine multiplied by any number less than 11 adds up to 9.

    9 x 3 = 27   (2 + 7 = 9)
    9 x 9 = 81   (8 + 1 = 9)

Division

$$6 \; / \; 3 \; = \; 2 \qquad\qquad 6 \div 3 \; = \; 2$$

$$\frac{6}{3} \; = \; 2 \qquad\qquad 3 \overline{)6}^{\,2}$$

The above equations have the same values and are very straightforward. It is important to know that the order of the numbers is significant in division (and subtraction). Different ordering of numbers will result in different answers. For example:

$$10 \; / \; 5 = 2 \qquad \text{different} \qquad 5 \; / \; 10 = 0.5$$

$$15 \div 5 = 3 \qquad \text{different} \qquad 5 \div 15 = 0.33$$

$$\frac{100}{10} = 10 \qquad \text{different} \qquad \frac{10}{100} = 0.1$$

$$10 \overline{)50}^{\,5} \qquad \text{different} \qquad 50 \overline{)10}^{\,0.2}$$

Simply put, division determines how many times a number will fit into another. Picture an auditorium with 100 chairs available. Several schools want to send 20 students to see a play in the auditorium. Now you need to determine how many schools can attend the play. This will require division.

By dividing 100 by 20 ($100 \div 20$) you come up with the number 5. Five schools can send 20 students to attend the play.

Long Division

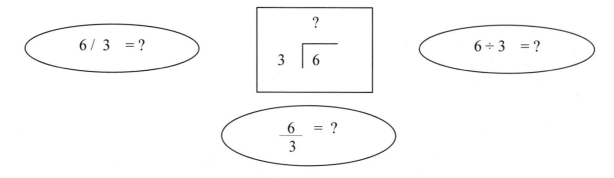

When performing long division, it is important to organize the information as is seen in the centre square. You have to understand how the different formats for division are transferred into the format seen above.

Example

$$2653 \div 7 = ?$$

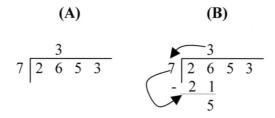

In order to answer a division question on paper, you must place the equation in the proper format. After this is accomplished you can begin to solve the problem.

(A)

The first step is to focus on the highlighted area of the number under the bracket. You have to work with a number that is larger than the dividing number (7). Because 2 is smaller than 7, you have to work with 26. Ask yourself how many times you can multiply 7 without going over 26. If you count by 7's (7, 14, 21, 28) you'll realize that 3 is the most times that 7 will fit into 26.

(B)

With the information you have in section A, you now have to perform a simple multiplication. Take the top number (3) and multiply it by the dividing number (7). The answer is placed below 26 and then subtracted from the digits you were working with. (26 - 21 = 5) Make sure you keep the numbers in the proper columns. (If, after subtracting, the answer is greater than the dividing number, you need to start again using a larger top number.)

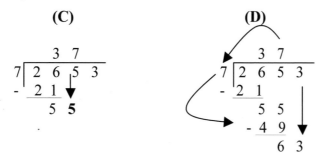

(C)

After subtraction, bring down the next digit to sit beside the solution. This becomes your new number to work with (55). Then repeat step A using this number. Determine how many times you can multiply 7 without exceeding 55. Place this digit above the next digit in the question on top of the bracket.

(D)

Next repeat step B. Multiply out the 7's and record your answer below the 55. Subtracting the numbers results in 6. Continue to work the same pattern, and bring down the next digit in the question to determine a new number to work with.

(E)

```
              3 7 9
        7 |2 6 5 3
          - 2 1
              5 5
            - 4 9
                6 3
              - 6 3
                  0
```

(E)

The final steps in the process are to repeat the process. Determine how many times you can multiply 7 without going over 63. You can do this 9 times. When you multiply it out and subtract the result is 0. The answer to the question is shown above.

$$2653 \div 7 = 379$$

Decimals

There are times when you are dividing a number and, after the final subtraction, there is a value left over. This is a remainder. When this happens, you can choose whether or not to continue calculating the number. If you continue, 1 or more decimal points will be introduced.

Example:

```
        3 3 1                         3 3 1.6 2 5
    8 ⌐2 6 5 3                    8 ⌐2 6 5 3.0 0 0
      - 2 4                           - 2 4
        2 5                             2 5
       - 2 4                           - 2 4
          1 3                             1 3
         - 0 8                           - 0 8
            5                               5 0
                                          - 4 8
                                             2 0
                                            - 1 6
                                               4 0
                                             - 4 0
                                                0
```

You must follow the same procedure with decimal places as you would with regular long division. Ensure that the digits are properly lined up, and continue adding 0's after the decimal places in the equation.

Decimals and Whole Numbers

You may be required to solve division problems with decimals already in place. Below are two examples of decimals occurring in division questions.

Example 1

```
                               7.1 7
  5 ⌐3 5 . 8 5          5 ⌐3 5 . 8 5
```

To answer the question correctly, you have to place the decimal point in the answer directly above the decimal point in the question.

Example 2

```
                               1 0 6 0 . 0
  2.7 ⌐2 8 6 2          27 ⌐2 8 6 2 0 . 0
```

When a decimal point is found in the denominator (the number of parts into which the whole is divided – bottom number of a fraction), then you must eliminate it before answering the question. This is achieved by shifting the decimal point however many spaces to the right it takes to create a whole number, in this example one space. This has to be matched by shifting the decimal place in the numerator (the number to be divided – top number of a fraction) by one space as well. If the numerator is a whole number, shift the decimal point right by adding a zero, as in the example above.

Example 3

$$3.5 \overline{)46.55} \qquad 35 \overline{)465.5}^{\,13.3}$$

When a decimal point is found in both the numerator and the denominator you must combine both steps. First, you must eliminate the decimal place in the denominator, as in example 2. Then you have to ensure that the new decimal place lines up, as in example 1.

Hints

Long division becomes more complicated with higher numbers, especially higher denominators.

$$67 \overline{)3015}^{\,0045}$$
$$\begin{array}{r} -268 \\ \hline 335 \\ -335 \\ \hline 0 \end{array}$$

Using 0's to Line up Numbers

67 will not fit into 3, or 30. You will therefore have to work with 301. By placing 0's above the 3 and the 0, (highlighted), you will not make any errors with improperly aligned numbers.

Rounding Up

Determining how many times 67 will fit into 301 can be a difficult task. It may help to round 67 up to 70. By counting 70 four times, you will reach 280. Five times equals 350, which exceeds 301. Four is the best guess, and by multiplying it out, using 67 you are proven correct.

Disregarding Decimals

The majority of the answers on a test will not require decimals. If your calculation of an equation gives you an answer with decimals, but none of the optional answers have decimals, stop calculating. Make a selection from the available options, or consider that you made a mistake. Quickly check your work, but don't spend too much time on one question that's causing you problems. Move onto the next question.

Zeros and Ones

Any time zero is divided by any other number the answer is 0.

$0 / 3 = 0$ $0 \div 25 = 0$ $\dfrac{0}{99} = 0$ $0\overline{)99}^{\;0}$

It is impossible for a number to be divided by 0. It is indefinable.

$9 / 0 = \text{undefined}$ $77 \div 0 = \text{undefined}$ $\dfrac{66}{0} = \text{undefined}$

Any number divided by 1 is equal to itself.

$3 / 1 = 3$ $55 \div 1 = 55$ $\dfrac{1{,}297}{1} = 1{,}297$ $1\overline{)38}^{\;38}$

Place Value

It is important to maintain proper place value of digits when performing mathematical calculations. You must be able to convert written numbers into digits. For example:

Two million, forty thousand and two	2,040,002
One and a half million	1,500,000
Ten thousand and ten	10,010

You can practice place value questions by answering questions such as the ones below:

a) Write a number that is 100 more than 4, 904.
b) Write a number that is 1000 less than 478, 243.
c) What number is one more than 9,999?
d) What is the value of 5 in the number 241, 598?
e) What figure is in the ten thousands place in 4,365,243?
f) What number is 30,000 less than 423,599?

The answers are listed below.

Place value is important when lining up numbers for addition and subtraction questions. For example:

$$15 + 1043 + 603 + 20,602 = \quad \begin{array}{r} 20,602 \\ 1,043 \\ 603 \\ \underline{15} \\ 22,263 \end{array}$$

$$13.09 + 0.4 + 206 + 0.002 = \quad \begin{array}{r} 206.000 \\ 13.090 \\ 0.400 \\ \underline{0.002} \\ 219.492 \end{array}$$

One of the most common errors is failing to place digits correctly under one another, which often occurs when trying to calculate these problems in your head.

Answers to practice questions.

a) 5,004	b) 477,243
c) 10,000	d) 500
e) 6	f) 393,599

Make sure you are comfortable with the proper names for the location of digits in a number.

1, 234, 567.890

1 = millions column

2 = hundred thousands column

3 = ten thousands column

4 = thousands column

5 = hundreds column

6 = tens column

7 = ones column

8 = tenths column

9 = hundredths column

0 = thousandths column

Order of Operations

The following rules have to be obeyed while working with mathematical equations. There is an order to how numbers are manipulated and worked on.

B E D M A S

You should memorize this acronym, as it tells you how to proceed with an equation.

1)   **B** – Brackets

You must perform all mathematical calculations that occur within brackets before any other calculation in the equation.

2)   **E** – Exponents

After calculations within brackets are handled, you have to perform any calculations with exponents next.

3)   **D / M** – Division and Multiplication

Division and multiplication components are next. These are handled in the order they appear reading from left to right.

4)   **A / S** – Addition and Subtraction

The final calculations are individual addition and subtraction questions, which are performed in the order they appear reading from left to right.

The best way to understand this process is to work through several problems.

Example 1:		
$6 + 5 \times 3 - 7$	Step 1: Multiplication	$5 \times 3 = 15$
$6 + 15 - 7$	Step 2: Addition	$6 + 15 = 21$
$21 - 7$	Step 3: Subtraction	$21 - 7 = 14$
Example 2:		
$14 - 7 + 18 \div 3$	Step 1: Division	$18 \div 3 = 6$
$14 - 7 + 6$	Step 2: Subtraction	$14 - 7 = 7$
$7 + 6$	Step 3: Addition	$7 + 6 = 13$

Example 3:

7 + (15 − 6 x 2)	Step 1: Brackets	6 x 2 = 12
7 + (15 − 12)	Remember to follow the order of operation within the brackets. (Multiply before subtracting.)	15 − 12 = 3
7 + 3	Step 2: Addition	7 + 3 = 10

Example 4:

2 (2 + 5) ²	Step 1: Brackets	2 + 5 = 7
2 (7) ²	Step 2: Exponents	7² = 7 x 7 = 49
2 (49)	Step 3: Multiplication	2 x 49 = 98

Remember that two numbers separated only by brackets are multiplied together (a bracket = x.)   2 (6) = 6 x 2

Practice Questions

Try these practice questions to see if you are comfortable with mathematical order of operation. The final answers are listed below.

a) $7 - 4 + 6 \times 8 \div 2$ b) $14 + 8 (6 - 3)$

c) $30 - 3(5 - 2)^2$ d) $(5 - 1) (4 + 7)$

e) $75 - (6 \div (2+1))^2$ f) $10^2 - 10 + 3^2$

g) $(10 + 3) \times 2 + 6(5-2)$ h) $17 + 6^2 (18 \div 9)$

i) $4 (5+2-3+6)$ j) $10 (6 + (15 - (10-5)))$

Answers

a) 27	b) 38	c) 3	d) 44
e) 71	f) 99	g) 44	h) 89
i) 40	j) 160		

Grouping Like Terms

You will come across mathematical problems where you have to group like terms together. Examples of this are very common with money. Whenever you are adding sums of money, there is no need to continually restate the same denominations. Below is an example of an equation adding up a suspect's money:

Denomination	# of Bills
$50	4
$20	3
$10	4

One means of calculating the total value of money seized is to individually add up all of the bills.

$$50 + 50 + 50 + 50 + 20 + 20 + 20 + 10 + 10 + 10 + 10$$

However, there is an easier and more orderly way of writing and working with this equation. Here is the statement rewritten separating the like terms.

$$(50 + 50 + 50 + 50) + (20 + 20 + 20) + (10 + 10 + 10 + 10)$$

Instead of adding all of the $50 bills together you can count the number of 50's and multiply that number by the value.

$$50 + 50 + 50 + 50 \quad = \quad 4 \times 50 \text{ or } 4 (50)$$
$$20 + 20 + 20 \quad = \quad 3 \times 20 \text{ or } 3 (20)$$
$$10 + 10 + 10 + 10 \quad = \quad 4 \times 10 \text{ or } 4 (10)$$

The statement can then be written more clearly as: $\quad 4(50) + 3 (20) + 4 (10)$

Remember that it doesn't matter what order the terms are in, so long as they remain together. The above equation could be restated any of the following ways:

$$3(20) + 4(50) + 4(10) \qquad 20(3) + 50(4) + 10(4)$$

$$20(3) + 10(4) + 50(4) \qquad 4(10) + 3(20) + 4(50)$$

Like terms can occur in any addition question. It doesn't have to be a monetary question. Any time you see two or more of the same number in an addition problem, they can be combined.

$$5 + 6 + 3 + 5 + 2 + 6 + 5 \quad = \quad 3(5) + 2(6) + 3 + 2$$

$$75 + 63 + 75 + 63 + 75 \quad = \quad 3(75) + 2(63)$$

$$5 + 5 + 5 + 5 + 5 + 4 \quad = \quad 5(5) + 4$$

Fractions

A fraction is simply a part of a whole thing. The example below is of a circle divided into four pieces. Each segment represents ¼ of the circle.

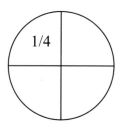

In each of the circles below, the same area is represented, but the area is divided into different numbers of equal parts.

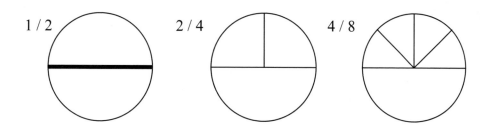

This diagram demonstrates that the fractions 1/2, 2/4 and 4/8 represent the same quantity.

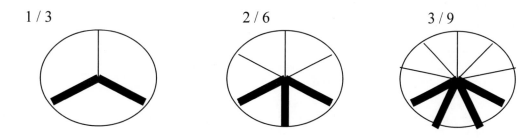

The fractions 1/3, 2/6 and 3/9 are equivalent. You can determine fractions of equivalent value by multiplying both the numerator and the denominator of the fraction by the same number.

$$\frac{1 \times 7}{3 \times 7} = \frac{7}{21} \qquad \text{thus} \qquad \frac{7}{21} = \frac{1}{3}$$

A similar rule holds when dividing the numerators and denominators of fractions. This is necessary to reduce fractions to their lowest form.

$$\frac{5 \text{ divided by } 5}{15 \text{ divided by } 5} = \frac{1}{3}$$

Improper Fractions

When a fraction has a larger numerator than denominator then the fraction is larger than one. The diagram below illustrates an example of improper fractions.

3 / 2   =   1 1/2

Adding and Subtracting Fractions

Whenever you are adding or subtracting fractions, you have to ensure that the denominators of the fractions are the same. For example:

$\frac{1}{2}$ + $\frac{6}{8}$ does not equal $\frac{7}{10}$

By multiplying both the denominator and the numerator of 1/2 by 4, you will be able to add the fractions together. 1 / 2 becomes 4 / 8.

$\frac{4}{8}$ + $\frac{6}{8}$ = $\frac{10}{8}$ = $\frac{5}{4}$

When you are adding and subtracting fractions, you also maintain the same denominator, and add or subtract the numerator.

$\frac{3}{4}$ - $\frac{1}{4}$ = $\frac{2}{4}$ = $\frac{1}{2}$ $\frac{3}{18}$ + $\frac{12}{18}$ = $\frac{15}{18}$ = $\frac{5}{6}$

$\frac{5}{10}$ - $\frac{3}{10}$ = $\frac{2}{10}$ = $\frac{1}{5}$ $\frac{7}{8}$ + $\frac{5}{8}$ = $\frac{12}{8}$ = 1 $\frac{1}{2}$

Multiplying Fractions

When multiplying fractions, there is no need to find a common denominator. Simply multiply the two top numbers and then multiply the two bottom numbers. Multiplying two fractions together (other than improper) will result in a fraction that is smaller than the original numbers.

$\frac{4}{5}$ x $\frac{3}{4}$ = $\frac{12}{20}$ = $\frac{3}{5}$ $\frac{1}{2}$ x $\frac{1}{5}$ = $\frac{1}{10}$

$\frac{3}{4}$ x $\frac{7}{18}$ = $\frac{21}{72}$ = $\frac{7}{24}$ $\frac{3}{2}$ x $\frac{4}{5}$ = $\frac{12}{10}$ = 1 $\frac{1}{5}$

Dividing Fractions

Division with fractions is very similar to multiplying with fractions.

12 divided by 12 = 1   12 goes into 12 once

12 divided by 6 = 2   6 goes into 12 twice

12 divided by 4 = 3   4 goes into 12 three times

12 divided by 3 = 4   3 goes into 12 four times

12 divided by 2 = 6   2 goes into 12 six times

12 divided by 1 = 12   1 goes into 12 twelve times

12 divided by 1/2 = 24   1/2 goes into 12 twenty four times

This is logical when you think about the statement on the right. Whenever you are dividing by a fraction you have to multiply one fraction by the reciprocal of the other. That is, when you divide one fraction by another, you have to multiply one fraction by the inverse of the other. For example:

$$\frac{1}{2} \div \frac{6}{7} = \frac{1}{2} \times \frac{7}{6} = \frac{7}{12}$$

$$\frac{3}{4} \div \frac{4}{5} = \frac{3}{4} \times \frac{5}{4} = \frac{15}{16}$$

$$1\frac{3}{4} \div \frac{4}{5} = \frac{7}{4} \times \frac{5}{4} = \frac{35}{16} = 2\frac{3}{16}$$

Whenever dividing mixed fractions (1 1/2, 2 3/4 etc) you must use improper fractions (3/2, 11/4 etc).

Percentages

It is important to have a solid background in decimals and fractions before you try to handle percentage questions. Percentages are simply fractions. Per means "out of" and cent means "a hundred". Percentages are fractions with 100 as a denominator. They are often noted with this sign: %.

10 % means 10 out of 100 or $\frac{10}{100}$

13 % means 13 out of 100 or $\frac{13}{100}$

100 % means 100 out of 100 or $\frac{100}{100}$

100% means everything. 100% of your salary is your whole salary. You simply follow the same rules of conversion from fractions to decimals for calculating percentages. Simply move the decimal points two places to the left to convert percents to decimals. This is essentially dividing the percentage by 100.

Example: 7 5 %   = 0 . 7 5

              8%   = 0 . 0 8

             5 3 . 5 % = 0 . 5 3 5

          2 0 8 %   = 2 . 0 8

Any percent larger than 100% indicates more than the whole. For example:

A man's stock portfolio is worth 125% of what it was a year ago. This means that the stocks are now worth 25% more. If his stocks were worth $500 last year, they would be worth:

$500 x 125% =
$$\begin{array}{r} 500 \\ \times\ 1.25 \\ \hline \$\ 625 \end{array}$$

Percentages with Fractions

Some questions you encounter may incorporate percentages and fractions. Examples include 2 1/2 % or 33 1/3 %. In order to deal with these problems, you must first convert the percentages to improper fractions.

$$2 \ 1/2 \ = \ 5/2 \qquad\qquad 33 \ 1/3 \ = \ 100/3$$

After this step you simply carry out the division question.

```
        2 . 5              3 3 . 3 3
    2 | 5 . 0          3 | 1 0 0 . 0 0
        4
        1 0
        1 0
          0
```

Once you have the decimal equivalent of the percentage, you then follow the same rules that apply to a regular percentage. Divide the number by 100 or, more simply, move the decimal to the left twice. Thus:

$$2 \ 1/2\% = 0.025 \qquad\qquad 33 \ 1/3\% = 0.3333$$

Percentages You Should Memorize

25%	=	1 / 4	=	0.25
50%	=	1 / 2	=	0.5
75%	=	3 / 4	=	0.75
100%	=	4 / 4	=	1.00
33 1/3 %	=	1 / 3	=	0.333
66 2/3 %	=	2 / 3	=	0.666
10%	=	1 / 10	=	0.1
20%	=	1 / 5	=	0.2
40%	=	2 / 5	=	0.4
60%	=	3 / 5	=	0.6
80%	=	4 / 5	=	0.8

Decimal / Fraction Conversion Instruction

Fraction to Decimal

There are many situations where you will have to convert fractions to decimals. Decimals are often easier to work with. Changing fractions to decimals is simply a division problem. All you have to do is take the numerator and divide it by the denominator.

Examples:

$$1/2 = 2\overline{\smash{)}\,1.0}$$
$$\,0.5$$
$$-1.0$$
$$0$$

$$4/5 = 5\overline{\smash{)}\,4.0}$$
$$\,0.8$$

$$1/3 = 3\overline{\smash{)}\,1.000}$$
$$\,0.333$$
$$-0.9$$
$$\overline{0.10}$$
$$-09$$
$$\overline{010}$$
$$-09$$
$$1$$

Mixed Fractions

Mixed fractions have to first be converted to improper fractions before they can be converted to decimals. Multiplying the whole number by the denominator and adding the numerator will achieve this. As soon as the improper fraction is found, you calculate the decimal in the same way as above.

Example 1

$$3\frac{1}{2} = \frac{7}{2} \qquad 2\overline{\smash{)}\,7.0} \quad 3.5$$

Multiply 3 by 2, and then add 1. This is the new numerator, and the denominator remains the same.

Example 2

$$2\frac{5}{6} = \frac{17}{6} \qquad 6\overline{\smash{)}\,17.000} \quad 2.833$$

Decimal to Fraction

When converting decimals to fractions, place value is extremely important. The first decimal point to the right of the decimal point is the tenths, followed by the hundredths, thousandths, etc. All you have to do is properly line up the place value with the proper denominator.

$$0.1 \quad \text{is a way of writing} \quad \frac{1}{10}$$

$$0.01 \quad \text{is a way of writing} \quad \frac{1}{100}$$

and

$$0.6 \quad \text{is a way of writing} \quad \frac{6}{10}$$

$$0.78 \quad \text{is a way of writing} \quad \frac{78}{100}$$

There is one zero in the denominator for every place to the right of the period in the original decimal.

Exponents

Exponents indicate how many times a number should be multiplied by itself. If a number is raised to the power of 2, the number should be multiplied by itself twice. If the number is raised to the power of 6, the number should be multiplied by itself 6 times.

$$2^2 = 2 \times 2 = 4$$

$$2^3 = 2 \times 2 \times 2 = 8$$

$$2^4 = 2 \times 2 \times 2 \times 2 = 16$$

$$2^5 = 2 \times 2 \times 2 \times 2 \times 2 = 32$$

$$7^2 = 7 \times 7 = 49$$

$$5^4 = 5 \times 5 \times 5 \times 5 = 625$$

Positive and Negative Integers

You must have an understanding of positive and negative integers and how they react when they are added, subtracted, multiplied and divided by each other. Look at the number line below. Positive integers exist to the right of the zero and negative integers exist to the left of the zero.

...-8 -7 -6 -5 -4 -3 -2 -1 0 1 2 3 4 5 6 7...

Adding Positive and Negative Integers

1) - 7 + 5 = -2   2) - 6 + 3 = -3
3) - 2 + 7 = 5   4) - 4 + 11 = 7

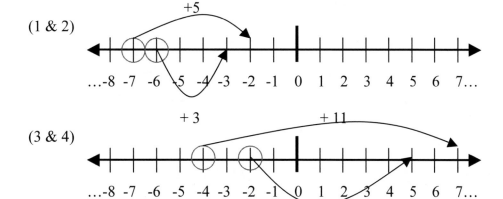

Subtracting Positive and Negative Integers

1) - 2 – 5 = -7   2) - 4 – 8 = -12
3) 4 – 7 = -3   4) 2 – 5 = -3

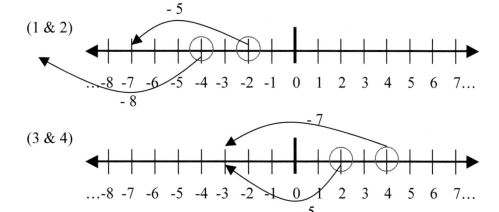

When adding and subtracting positive and negative integers you must know what to do when two signs are directly beside each other.

2 Positives	**2 Negatives**	**Opposite Signs**
+ + = +	- - = +	+ - = -

For instance:

	6 + (+3)	6 + (-3)	6 - (-3)
	= 6 + 3	= 6 – 3	= 6 + 3
	= 9	= 3	= 9

Try these sample questions. The answers are below.

1) 5 – 9 =   2) – 4 + 6 =   3) – 5 – 2 =   4) 2 – 7 =

5) –2 + 5 =   6) 1 – 9 =   7) 4 – (+6) =   8) –2 –(-4) =

9) + 3 – (-6) =   10) 6 + (-4) =   11) 6 + (+2) =   12) -3 + (-2) =

Multiplying and Dividing Positive and Negative Integers

While multiplying and dividing positive and negative integers, remember the rules that apply to adding and subtracting integers with two signs directly beside each other.

2 Positives	**2 Negatives**	**Opposite Signs**
+ + = +	- - = +	+ - = -

You should break questions like this into two steps.

Step 1: Solve the equation ignoring the signs.

6 x (-3) = 18	- 5 x 4 = 20
5 x (-7) = 35	- 3 x (-4) = 12
-12 ÷ (-4) = 3	-21 ÷ 3 = 7
36 ÷ (-9) = 4	-64 ÷ (-8) = 8

If you ignored the + and – signs in front of the numbers you would end up with the answers above.

Step 2: Determine the + / - sign. The rules about + / - integers come into play. If there are two + signs, then the equation is positive. If there are two – signs, then the equation is also positive. If there is one + and one – sign, then the equation is negative.

$$6 \times (-3) = \mathbf{-18} \quad (+ / -) \qquad\qquad -5 \times 4 = \mathbf{-20} \quad (- / +)$$
$$5 \times (-7) = \mathbf{-35} \quad (- / +) \qquad\qquad -3 \times (-4) = \mathbf{12} \quad (- / -)$$
$$-12 \div (-4) = \mathbf{3} \quad (- / -) \qquad\qquad -21 \div 3 = \mathbf{-7} \quad (- / +)$$
$$36 \div (-9) = \mathbf{-4} \quad (+ / -) \qquad\qquad -64 \div (-8) = \mathbf{8} \quad (- / -)$$

The final answers are displayed in bold above.

Try these sample questions. The answers are posted below.

a) $3 \times (-6) =$ b) $-2 \times (-9) =$ c) $-18 \div (-9) =$

d) $7 \times 7 =$ e) $-72 \div 8 =$ f) $-12 \times (-9) =$

g) $7 \times (-6) =$ h) $-28 \div (-4) =$ i) $16 \div (-4) =$

j) $3 \times (-4) =$ k) $-45 \div (-15) =$ l) $-3 \times (2) =$

Answers to Sample Questions

1) $5 - 9 = \mathbf{-4}$ 2) $-4 + 6 = \mathbf{2}$ 3) $-5 - 2 = \mathbf{-7}$

4) $2 - 7 = \mathbf{-5}$ 5) $-2 + 5 = \mathbf{3}$ 6) $1 - 9 = \mathbf{-8}$

7) $4 - (+6) = \mathbf{-2}$ 8) $-2 - (-4) = \mathbf{2}$ 9) $+3 - (-6) = \mathbf{9}$

10) $6 + (-4) = \mathbf{2}$ 11) $6 + (+2) = \mathbf{8}$ 12) $-3 + (-2) = \mathbf{-5}$

_____

a) $3 \times (-6) = \mathbf{-18}$ b) $-2 \times (-9) = \mathbf{18}$ c) $-18 \div (-9) = \mathbf{2}$

d) $7 \times 7 = \mathbf{49}$ e) $-72 \div 8 = \mathbf{-9}$ f) $-12 \times (-9) = \mathbf{108}$

g) $7 \times (-6) = \mathbf{-42}$ h) $-28 \div (-4) = \mathbf{7}$ i) $16 \div (-4) = \mathbf{-4}$

j) $3 \times (-4) = \mathbf{-12}$ k) $-45 \div (-15) = \mathbf{3}$ l) $-3 \times (2) = \mathbf{-6}$

Perimeters

Perimeter is defined as the border around an object, or the outside edge of an object.

Perimeter is calculated by adding the sides of the object together.

Perimeter = 6 + 5 + 5 + 5+ 5 + 6
          = 32

Perimeter = 4 + 4 + 4 + 4
          = 16

Perimeter = 3 + 3 + 4
          = 10

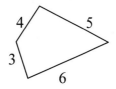

Perimeter = 3 + 4 + 5 + 6
          = 18

Circumferences

Circumference is also defined as the border around a shape, but is always associated with a circle.

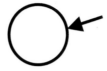

In order to determine the circumference of a circle, you must use a formula. You need to be familiar with some definitions.

$$\pi = 3.14 \ (\text{pi})$$

You are going to have to remember that pi is equal to 3.14.

Diameter (d)

Diameter is the distance from one edge of the circle, through the middle, to the opposite side of the circle.

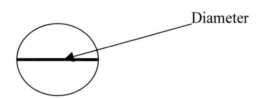

Radius (r)

Radius is defined as ½ of the diameter, or the distance from the mid-point of a circle to its outer edge.

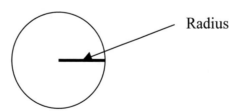

Formula for Calculating Circumference

$$C = 2 \times (\pi) \times r \qquad \text{or} \qquad C = d \times (\pi)$$

$$C = 2 \times (3.14) \times 5$$

$$= 31.4 \text{ cm}$$

$$C = 10 \times (3.14)$$

$$= 31.4 \text{ cm}$$

The information you are given in a question will dictate the formula you should use to calculate the circumference. If you are given the radius, calculate the diameter by multiplying by two. Dividing the diameter by two will give you the radius.

Areas

Area is space that is occupied within the borders of a shape. It is measured in units squared and is represented by the area shaded in the shapes below.

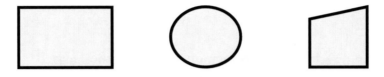

The three shapes you should know how to calculate area for are the triangle, rectangle and circle.

Area of a Rectangle or Square

To calculate the area of a square or rectangle, multiply the base of the object by its' height.

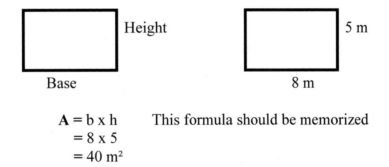

$A = b \times h$ This formula should be memorized
$= 8 \times 5$
$= 40 \text{ m}^2$

Area of a Triangle

To calculate the area of a triangle, follow the formula below.

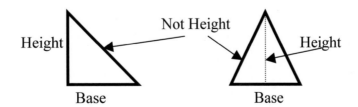

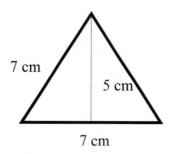

7 cm

5 cm

7 cm

$A = \frac{1}{2} \times b \times h$ **This formula should be memorized.**
$= \frac{1}{2} \times 7 \times 5$
$= 17.5 \text{ cm}^2$

Remember that height is not necessarily an edge of the triangle, but the distance from the base to the top of the triangle.

Area of a Circle

To calculate the area of a circle, follow the formula below.

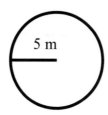

5 m

$A = \pi\,(r)^2$ **This formula should be memorized.**
$= (3.14)\,(5)^2$
$= (3.14)\,(25)$
$= 78.5 \text{ m}^2$

Other Shapes

You may have to calculate the area of shapes other than basic squares, triangles and circles. You can attempt to break shapes into smaller components and use the formulas above. For example:

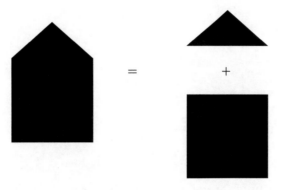

Calculate the area of the triangle and adding it to the area of the square results in the area of the whole shape.

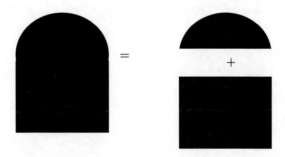

You can divide the shape on the left into a square and a half circle. Calculate the area of the square and the area of the circle. Divide the area of the circle in half and add the two together.

Volumes

Volume is defined as the area occupied by a three dimensional shape. If you pictured an empty cup, volume is the amount of liquid it contains. Calculating volume for different objects can be very difficult and involves complex formulas. We will discuss how to calculate the volume of three simple objects. Volume is always discussed in units cubed (example $3m^3$.)

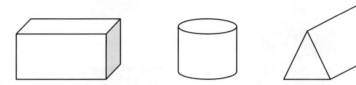

Volume of a Cube

You should memorize the formula for calculating the volume of a cube.

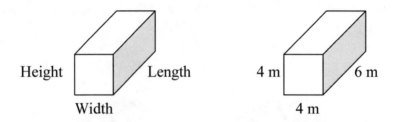

$$V = \text{length x width x height}$$
$$= 6 \text{ x } 4 \text{ x } 4$$
$$= 96 \text{ m}^3$$

Volume of a Cylinder

To calculate the volume of a cylinder, determine the area of the circle and multiply it by the height of the cylinder.

Radius = 5 m

Height = 10 m

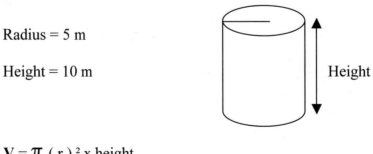

$$V = \pi \, (r)^2 \text{ x height}$$
$$= (3.14) \, (5)^2 \, (10)$$
$$= 785 \text{ m}^3$$

Volume of a Triangular Shaped Object

To calculate the volume of an object like the one below, first calculate the area of the triangle and multiply it by the height of the object.

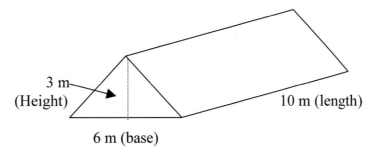

$$V = \tfrac{1}{2}\,(\text{base})\,(\text{height})\,(\text{length})$$
$$= \tfrac{1}{2}\,(6)\,(3)\,(10)$$
$$= 90 \text{ m}^3$$

Metric Conversions

The key to understanding metric conversions is to memorize the prefixes and roots to each word. The root of each word indicates the basic measurement (litre, metre, gram), while the prefixes determine the relative size of the measurement (larger or smaller units – milli, centi, kilo, etc,).

Prefixes

All units in the metric system are easily converted because they are all based on units of 10. When converting between different measurements of the same base unit, it is as easy as shifting the decimal point.

For example:

432,000 millimetres
43,200 centimetres   ALL EQUAL EACH OTHER
432 metres
0.432 kilometres

Length

Length is used to measure the distance between points. The base unit for length is the metre. The most common units you'll encounter with length include:

Millimetres – small units (25 millimetres in 1 inch)
Centimetres – small units (2.5 centimetres in 1 inch)
Metres – larger units (1 metre = 3.2 feet or 1.1 yards)
Kilometres – large units (1.6 kilometres in 1 mile)

Prefix	Example	Sign	Conversion
Milli	Millimetres	mm	1 m = 1000 mm
Centi	Centimetre	cm	1 m = 100 cm
Deci	Decigram	dm	1 m = 10 dm
-	Metre	m	1 m = 1 m
Kilo	Kilometre	km	1 km = 1000 m

Volume

Volume is defined as the capacity of a given container. It usually measures the amount of liquid or gas that an object can hold. For example, the volume of a pop can is 355 millilitres, or the volume of a milk carton is 1 litre. The base unit for volume in the metric system is the litre. A litre is roughly the amount of milk that will fit into a milk carton or roughly three glasses of milk.

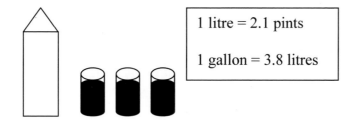

1 litre = 2.1 pints

1 gallon = 3.8 litres

The most common prefix used with volume is the millilitre (used to measure small amounts, such as tablespoons.) The majority of the time when measuring volume you will be using the litre measurement itself.

Prefix	Example	Sign	Conversion
Milli	Millilitres	mL	1 L = 1000 mL
Centi	Centilitres	cL	1 L = 100 cL
Deci	Decilitres	dL	1 L = 10 dL
-	Litres	L	1 L = 1 L
Kilo	Kilolitres	kL	1 kL = 1000 L

Mass or Weight

The base unit for weight in the metric system is the gram. The most common units you'll encounter with weight are:

Milligrams – very small (1000 milligrams in 1 gram)
Grams – small units (28.3 grams in 1 ounce)
Kilograms – large units (1 kilogram = 2.2 pounds)

Prefix	Example	Sign	Conversion
Milli	Milligrams	mg	1 g = 1000 mg
Centi	Centigram	cg	1 g = 100 cg
Deci	Decigram	dg	1 g = 10 dg
-	Gram	G	1 g = 1 g
Kilo	Kilogram	kg	1 kg = 1000 g

Algebraic Equations

Before beginning this section, make sure that you are comfortable with the rules of order of operation in mathematical equations. It is necessary to know in what order you add, subtract, divide and multiply in an equation.

Algebraic equations involve using letters and symbols to represent unknown numbers. In order to solve these equations you must isolate the unknown variable. We will begin with a couple of simple examples.

When solving algebraic equations, it is important to know the opposite mathematical operations. For example, subtraction is the opposite of addition and division is the opposite of multiplication. Square roots are the opposite of squaring. We will not cover square roots in this section.

$6 + y = 12$

$6 + y - 6 = 12 - 6$

$y = 6$

> In order to isolate the "y", eliminate a + 6 on the left hand side of the equation. In algebraic equations, whatever you do to one side of the equation you must also do to the other side. Subtract 6 from both sides.

$y - 3 = 15$

$y - 3 + 3 = 15 + 3$

$y = 18$

> In order to isolate the "y", eliminate a - 3 on the left hand side of the equation. Add 3 to both sides.

$7y = 42$

$7y / 7 = 42 / 7$

$y = 6$

> In this case, "y" is multiplied by 7. To eliminate a number that is being multiplied, divide by the same number. Divide both sides by 7.

$y / 12 = 5$

$y / 12 \times 12 = 5 \times 12$

$y = 60$

> In this case, "y" is divided by 12. To eliminate a number that is being divided, multiply by the same number. Multiply both sides by 12.

Practice solving some of these simple equations:

1) $y / 11 = 23$ 2) $15 + y = 63$ 3) $-5 + y = 10$

4) $13 (y) = 130$ 5) $5 y = 15$ 6) $6 + 3 + y = 56$

7) $2(y) = 56$ 8) $y / 8 = 4$ 9) $y (24) = 72$

Answers are below.

More Advanced Algebraic Equations

When solving equations, follow the order of operations which dictate that you perform equations within brackets, followed by exponents, then division and multiplication, and finally addition and subtraction. When isolating unknown variables, use the opposite order. We will not cover solving equations with exponents at this level.

$6 y + 12 = 84$

$6 y + 12 - \mathbf{12} = 84 - \mathbf{12}$

$6 y = 72$

$6 y / \mathbf{6} = 72 / \mathbf{6}$

$y = 12$

> In order to isolate the "y", first eliminate a + 12 on the left hand side of the equation. Subtract 12 from both sides. You are left with 6y = 12.
> To isolate "y", now simply divide both sides of the equation by 6.

$y / 3 + 12 - 2 = \mathbf{15 \times 3} + 4$

$y / 3 + 12 - 2 = 45 + \mathbf{4}$

$y / 3 + 12 - 2 = 49$

$y / 3 + 12 - 2 + \mathbf{2} = 49 + \mathbf{2}$

$y / 3 + 12 = 51$

$y / 3 + 12 - \mathbf{12} = 51 - \mathbf{12}$

$y / 3 = 39$

$y / 3 \times \mathbf{3} = 39 \times \mathbf{3}$

$y = 117$

> You may encounter equations where one side has operations without an unknown variable. In cases like this, solve the side without an unknown variable FOLLOWING THE STANDARD ORDER OF OPERATION RULES.
>
> After you have accomplished this, solve the equation in the standard manner. People more advanced in math will be able to consolidate portions of the left side as well, but unless you are comfortable you should proceed the way outlined to the left.

$(6 - y) \times 3 = 24$

$(6 - y) \times 3 / \mathbf{3} = 24 / \mathbf{3}$

$(6 - y) = 8$

$6 - y - \mathbf{6} = 8 - \mathbf{6}$

$-y = 2$

$-y \times \mathbf{(-1)} = 2 \times \mathbf{(-1)}$

$y = -2$

> Perform this equation following the standard rules. Leave the brackets until the end. When only the brackets remain, you can get rid of them as they no longer serve a purpose.
>
> When you are left with an equation where the unknown is isolated, but negative, simply multiply both sides of the equation by -1 to inverse the signs.
>
> The end result is that $y = -2$.

$18 / y = 2$

$18 / y \times \mathbf{(y)} = 2 \times \mathbf{(y)}$

$18 = 2y$

$18 / \mathbf{2} = 2y / \mathbf{2}$

$9 = y$

> One other tricky situation you may encounter is when "y" appears on the bottom of a division equation. In order to solve for "y", move it from the bottom of the division sign by multiplying both sides of the equation by "y". The result is $18 = 2y$. Now solve the rest of the equation.

WHATEVER YOU DO TO ONE SIDE OF AN EQUATION YOU MUST ALSO DO TO THE OTHER SIDE.

More Practice Questions

a) $3(y) + 6 - 10 = 89$

b) $(y) / 6 + 24 - 2 = 14$

c) $-y(3) + 55 = 105$

d) $5y - 32 = 24(3)$

e) $-32 + 6y/2 = 64$

f) $22y + 16(8) = 6y$

Answers:

1) 253	2) 48	3) 15
4) 10	5) 3	6) 47
7) 28	8) 32	9) 3

a) 31	b) -48	c) -16.7
d) 20.8	e) 32	f) -8

Teaching Material English

Common Grammar Errors

It is beyond the scope of this book to cover all grammar errors that can occur during a government examination. Below are merely some examples you may come across. If you feel your grammar is a significant barrier to landing the job, it would be prudent to review a grammar textbook, or perhaps take an English grammar course.

The Use of "Then" and "Than"

Then is used to indicate time. It has the same meaning as "afterwards", "subsequently" or "followed by".

> Ex: I went to the play, **and then** I went home.

Than is used in comparison. It can be used with the word "rather". It has the same meaning as "as opposed to", or "instead of".

> Ex: I would rather play baseball **than** hockey.

The Use of "Is When"

This is not correct. Use the term "occurs when."

> Ex: The best part of the movie **occurs when** the killer is revealed.

Subordinate Clauses

Be careful with subordinate clauses. If one clause has less emphasis (less importance) in a sentence, it is subordinate or dependent on the other clause. When these clauses occur at the beginning of the sentence, they can be tricky.

> Ex: **Since you began training,** you have been unable to work an entire shift.

If you rearrange the sentence you can understand how "since" acts as the conjunction.

> Ex: You have been able to work an entire shift **since you began training.**

Forming Plurals

It is difficult to determine the plural form of many words. Examples include:

Goose	Geese	Man	Men
Woman	Women	Mouse	Mice
Mother-in-Law	Mothers-in-Law		

Comparative Adjectives and Adverbs

Single Syllable Words:

To form the comparative adjective or adverb for most single syllable words, add "**-er**" to the end of the word. If there are three or more parties to compare, use the ending "**-est**."

Rafik was strong.	Sean is fast.
Bill was *stronger* than Rafik.	Sean is the faster of the two.
Pratik was the *strongest* of the three.	Sean is the fastest of the three.

Be careful. There are always exceptions to the rule in the English language. You should be able to tell by the sound of the words when you should use an alternative method of comparison.

I had a fun time at the party this year.
I had *more fun* this year than last year.
I had the *most fun* this year compared to all the other parties.

The words "funner" and "funnest" do not exist.

Multiple Syllable Words:

As with the example "fun", multiple syllable words use linking words while making comparisons. When comparing two parties, use the word "*more*"; and while comparing three or more parties, use the word "*most*".

He was *more eager* than her to finish the project.
He was the *most eager* of the three to finish the project.

Shelley was *more intelligent* than Michael.
Lucy was the *most intelligent* of the group.

Subject / Verb Agreement

It is important to make sure that the verb agrees with the noun it relates to. There are six types of persons in the English language:

I	We
You (singular)	You (plural)
He / She / It	They

In English, there are several ways that subjects and verbs relate to each other. Here are a couple:

I	*run / do / was*	We	*run / do / were*
You	*run / do / was*	You	*run / do / were*
He / She / It	*runs / does / was*	They	*run / do / were*

Be careful of confusing the subject and verb agreement.

Example: I run fast. I do well. I **don't** understand.
  He runs fast. He does well. He **doesn't** understand.

This can be difficult if there is a clause between the subject and the verb. When analyzing a sentence, try to read the sentence without the clause to determine if there is subject / verb agreement.

Example: *Dheena*, along with the rest of us, *does* well.
Read aloud: *Dheena does well.* "Dheena do well" doesn't sound right.

The Use of "It's" and "Its"

This is often wrongly expressed.
"It's" is a contraction that translates into "it is".

> *It's* getting late. = *It is* getting late.
> I'm tired and *it's* time to go. = I'm tired and *it is* time to go.

"Its" refers to possession. It is the equivalent to an apostrophe "s".

The train and all *its* passengers were safe.
The train and all **the train's** passengers were safe.

The Use of "There", "Their" and "They're"

These are also often confused. Here are the definitions:

> There: a location, nearby, in attendance, present
>   The book is over **there,** on the table.

> Their: a possessive pronoun implying ownership, belonging to them,
>   I took **their** advice and followed through with the job.

> They're: a contraction, meaning "they are"
>   **They're** going to arrive late because of the snow.

The Use of "Two", "To", and "Too"

Make sure you follow these definitions. Use the correct "to/too/two" in the proper place.

> <u>To</u>: in the direction, toward, near, in order to.
> I went **to** the store **to** buy some bread.

> <u>Too</u>: also, as well, in addition, besides, and excessively.
> The teacher handed out an "A" to Bill and to Cindy, **too.**
> Shayna and Jeff just left **too**.
> The pizza deliverer took **too** long, so the pizza was free.

> <u>Two</u>: the number
> There were **two** beavers sitting on the log.

Verb Tenses

When reading a passage, ensure that the verbs in a sentence agree and that verbs discussing the same idea are in the same tense. For example, if you are speaking in the past in one sentence, you must remain consistent in the sentence following.

> Incorrect
> Bill **ran** to the store very quickly. He **is taking** Sally with him.
> Sean **reads** at a fourth grade level and **studied** very hard.

> Correct:
> Bill **ran** to the store very quickly. He **took** Sally with him.
> Sean **reads** at a fourth grade level and **studies** very hard.

Adverbs and Adjectives

Adverbs are used to modify or compliment verbs, adjectives or other adverbs. They generally explain how (gently), when (soon), or where (fully). A common trait of adverbs is to end in "*-ly*". However, this is not a reliable way to tell adverbs and adjectives apart.

Adjectives are used with nouns to describe a quality or modify a meaning. (old, tall, curly, Canadian, my, this...)

If the word you are describing or modifying is a noun, make sure you use the adjective form of the word. If the word is a verb, adjective, or adverb, use the adverb format.

He ran **quickly** down the street.	- Adverb quickly (how he runs)
He was a very **quick** thinker.	- Adjective quick (describing the thinker)
It was a **very large** house.	- Adverb very (describing large)
	- Adjective large (describing house)

| It was a **loud** song. | - Adjective loud (describing song) |
| She sang **loudly**. | - Adverb loudly (modifying sang) |

Uses of Commas in Lists

When a list is presented in a sentence, use commas between list items and a conjunction to separate the last two items on the list. It is not wrong to add an additional comma before the conjunction, but it is unnecessary.

He was going to bring his **toys, clothes, books and cookies** to class.

Angela was going to the Maritimes by **plane, train or boat**.

Uses of the Apostrophe

Apostrophes are used to indicate ownership.

Bill's school was one of the best in the country. (the school to which Bill went)
Martha's mirror was cracked. (the mirror belonging to Martha)

Meanings of "Fair" and "Fare"

People often confuse these two words. Definitions are listed below.

Fair: just, reasonable, light, fair haired, pale

He was a **fair** judge and handed down reasonable sentences.
The boy was very **fair**, and would burn easily in the sun.

Fare: charge, price, ticket, tariff, passenger

The **fare** for the plane was rather steep.

Subject / Object Noun Agreements

Depending on its role in the sentence, pronouns take on different forms. Below is a list.

Subject		**Object**	
I	We	Me	Us
You	You	You	You
He / She / It	They	Him / Her / It	Them

If the pronoun is acting as a subject, use a subject pronoun.

Subject	**Object**
Tim and I went to the baseball game.	Tim threw the ball to me.
He was the last one to leave.	Shayna surprised her at the party.
They will come later.	Alex passes the gravy to them.

The major distinction between a subject and an object is the manner in which the verb relates to the pronouns. A subject tends to perform the verb, while an object tends to have the verb performed on it. Read the examples above and see if you understand the difference. If not, you will have to check with a grammar textbook.

Double Negatives

Avoid using double negatives when both speaking and writing,. Examples include:

I do **not** want **no** gum.	I do **not** want **any** gum.
You ca**n't** go to **no** store.	You ca**n't** go to **any** store.
The sergeant has**n't no** time.	The sergeant has**n't any** time.

The uses of "From" and "Off"

When receiving objects, goods or information, remember that the word "from" is correct even though in common spoken language we often use the word "off".

The doctor received the X-rays **from** the technician.
She pulled the book **from** the cupboard.

The Uses of "Stayed" and "Stood"

This is similar to the "From" and "Off" problem mentioned above. You often hear the word "stood" used in spoken language, but "stayed" is the correct word to use.

Stood is the past tense of stand (position, place, locate). Stayed is the past tense of stay (remain, wait, reside.)

I should have stayed with my fellow officers in the tough times.
The nurse stayed by the patient all night long.

The Use of Amount and Number

Generally speaking, we use **"amount"** with something that is measured or can't be counted, such as weights or volumes. We use **"number"** to describe quantities that are countable.

She had a large **amount** of liquid in the test tube.
There was a large **amount** of chocolate used in the recipe.
There were a large **number** of soldiers in the army.
The **number** of signs on the highway is enormous.

Run-On Sentences

Watch out for run-on sentences when writing. When two or more separate independent clauses are incorrectly joined, this is a run-on sentence. An independent clause is the part of a sentence that could stand alone. If you put a period at the end of an independent clause, it could serve as a sentence.

Here is an example of a run-on sentence:

Jamie was extremely angry when he missed his final chemistry exam, he went back to his dormitory and yelled at his roommate for failing to wake him up.

There are several ways to deal with a run-on sentence.

1) Make two Separate Sentences.

This is the easiest way to correct the problem. Simply add a period and start the second sentence with a capital letter.

> Correct:
> Jamie was extremely angry when he missed his final chemistry exam. He went back to his dormitory and yelled at his roommate for failing to wake him up.

2) Use a semicolon to separate the independent clauses.

Semicolons can often replace periods, but a comma can't. Do not capitalize the word immediately after a semicolon.

> Correct:
> Jamie was extremely angry when he missed his final chemistry exam; he went back to his dormitory and yelled at his roommate for failing to wake him up.

3) Use a subordinating conjunction with one of the clauses.

A subordinating conjunction is used to turn one of the clauses from an independent clause to a dependent clause. Examples of subordinating conjunctions include "because" and "since".

> Correct:
> Since Jamie was extremely angry when he missed his final chemistry exam, he went back to his dormitory and yelled at his roommate for failing to wake him up.

4) Use a comma and a coordinating conjunction between the two clauses.

Coordinating conjunctions can connect two clauses. The most common coordinating conjunctions include "and", "or", "but", and "so".

> Correct:
> Jamie was extremely angry when he missed his final chemistry exam, so he went back to his dormitory and yelled at his roommate for failing to wake him up.

5) Use a semicolon, conjunctive adverb and comma to separate the clauses.

Conjunctive adverbs can connect clauses. Examples of these adverbs include: "therefore", "moreover", "however", and "nonetheless". In order to properly use these adverbs, place a semicolon before the adverb and a comma after the adverb.

> Incorrect:
> Jamie was extremely angry when he missed his final chemistry exam, therefore he went back to his dormitory and yelled at his roommate for failing to wake him up.

> Correct:
> Jamie was extremely angry when he missed his final chemistry exam; therefore, he went back to his dormitory and yelled at his roommate for failing to wake him up.

Sentence Fragments

A sentence fragment is an incomplete sentence. There are two ways to change a sentence fragment to a complete sentence.

1) Add Words

Incorrect:
> Justin, running across the front lawn and enjoying his childhood days.
> (incomplete sentence)

Correct:
> Justin was running across the front lawn and enjoying his childhood days.
> (complete sentence)

2) Take Away Words

Creating a complete sentence from a sentence fragment can also be achieved by removing words from the sentence fragment.

Incorrect:
> While Trevor was completing the exam but having difficulty coming up with the answer to question #51.

Correct:

Trevor was completing the exam but having difficulty coming up with the answer to question #51.

Other Common Grammar Errors

Attend -	go to, be present at, concentrate
Tend -	be inclined, be likely, to have a tendency
Lose -	misplace, unable to find, to be defeated
Loose -	unfastened, wobbly, slack, movable
Threw -	hurled, tossed, past tense of "to throw"
Through -	from first to last, during, in the course of
Weather -	the seasons, elements, temperatures
Whether -	question of if, introducing an alternative possibility
Bear -	an animal in the woods, or to tolerate, stand, put up with
Bare -	to expose, naked, uncovered

Teaching Material General

Observation and Memory

Memory

Developing your memory is a skill like any other, and will improve the more you practice. There are several methods to go about doing this.

1) Practice as many of the practice tests as possible to become familiar with the methods used during the real exam.
2) Practice reading passages and pictures in newspapers and magazines. Focus on names, and test yourself 30 minutes later to see how you did.
3) Have a friend note the makes, colours, and license plates of a few cars in an area and test yourself 30 minutes later.
4) Form pictures or links in your mind to assist your memory. For example, if you see a mug shot of a person that reminds you of your friend, link that friend to the mug shot in order to memorize it. Here is an example using license plates.

954 PNY   - remember 954 **P**eople in **N**ew **Y**ork
651 ZTZ   - remember 651 **Z**ee **T**ea**Z**e (the tease)
421 PLM   - remember 421 **PL**u**M**ber

Do whatever works for you. (Psychologists have found that by making expressions graphic, people remember them more easily.)

Observation

The observations and mapping questions are skills that can only be developed through repetitive practice. Tips to improve your observation skills include:

1) Take the practice exams in this book (or on the website) to become familiar with the testing process.

2) Purchase "spot the difference" puzzles.

3) Do word find puzzles in local papers.

4) Practice Mapping questions with friends using local maps, or building schematics.

Facial Visualization Questions

Facial visualization questions are common in entrance exams. They test your powers of observation and ability to spot similarities and differences between suspects that look alike. This is a necessary skill for a peace officer, as you will be asked to locate suspects with vague descriptions, or you may be dealing with an old photo or need to visualize what a suspect would look like with glasses, facial hair, etc.

Assume that the suspect's facial appearance has not changed in any permanent way. For example, a suspect might comb his or her hair differently, put on glasses, wear a different hat or grow facial hair. Any changes to bone structure, weight or facial features that would require plastic surgery should be excluded.

Which of the following four suspects matches the man shown above?

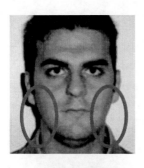 

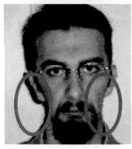 

You should focus on areas of the face that are difficult to change. As the circles demonstrate in the first and third photos, there seems to be an inconsistency with the cheek structure and general shape of the jaw. The jaw is too wide in the first photo and too narrow in the third. The fourth photo is a close match but the nose is not the right shape.

Some of the tests will use actual photographs of suspects, while others will use cartoon drawings of suspects. The same principles apply. Focus on:

- Shape of the head   - Shape of the chin
- Shape and placement of the eyes   - Shape of the cheeks
- Shape of the nose

Try to overlook or disregard any easy changes that a suspect can make to his/her appearance, such as:

Change in hairstyle   Glasses   Jewellery
Change in facial hair   Hats

Eliminate as Many Choices as Possible, then Guess

You will not be penalized if you guess incorrectly in these tests. Because there is a time limit, you must be efficient and use your time optimally. Don't waste too much time on one question. Look at your four options, eliminate as many as possible, and then guess which of the remaining ones is best. Remember, the questions will get more difficult throughout the test, so expect to spend more time on later questions than on the earlier ones.

Judgement Section

Framework for Analysis

It is important to have a framework for how you will approach judgement questions during an examination process. You must know how to establish hierarchies in order to prioritize activities and handle conflicting job requirements. Below is a possible value hierarchy that can be used to resolve difficult decisions.

1) Protection of Life and Limb.
This is an officers' first priority and supersedes all other decisions. This includes the lives of officers as well.

2) Obeying Orders in Emergency Situations
Officers have to be able to follow instructions even though they may not fully understand the justification for them.

3) Protection of Property
This is a primary duty of officers.

4) Performing other Required Duties
Officers then must act as required to keep the peace, enforce the law, and maintain order.

Remember that while you are performing your duties, your priorities include:

1) Assisting Endangered People (including victims of crime, injured people, etc.)

2) Keeping the Peace (calming disorder, preventing destruction)

3) Enforcing the Law (fairly and impartially)

4) Maintaining Order (investigating suspicious events, working with community members, correcting traffic problems)

5) Assisting Others Who Need Help (disabled, children, elderly, etc.)

Core Competencies

Review the list of core competencies found in the resume section. Remember that officer safety is paramount.

Pattern Solving

When you are attempting to solve patterns, be very observant and look for consistent changes and developments. These changes can include, but are not exclusive to:

1) Number of objects
2) Size of objects
3) Colour of objects
4) Shape of objects
5) Rotation / Flip of objects
6) Number of unique identifying marks

There are a number of different clues you must look for. The only way to improve your skills for this stage of the exam is to practice the puzzles in this book, on the website or puzzle books you may find in bookstores.

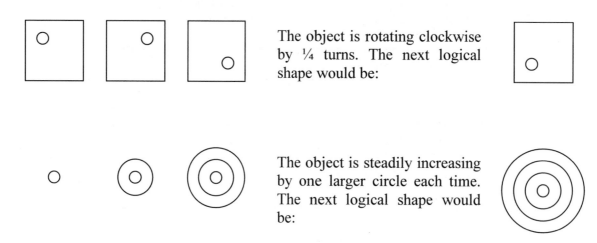

The object is rotating clockwise by ¼ turns. The next logical shape would be:

The object is steadily increasing by one larger circle each time. The next logical shape would be:

Sometimes you have to ignore information to detect the pattern.

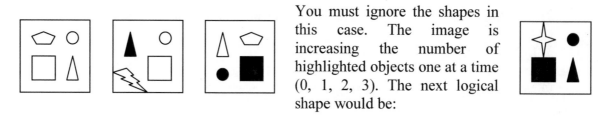

You must ignore the shapes in this case. The image is increasing the number of highlighted objects one at a time (0, 1, 2, 3). The next logical shape would be:

Spatial Folding Section

A common test used for measuring a person's spatial reasoning is ability involves measuring the ability to transfer flattened two-dimensional objects into three-dimensional objects by folding the object along dotted lines.

Folding Questions

These types of tests are used in the GATB. They are designed to measure your ability to transform a 2-dimensional diagram into a 3-dimensional object by folding the object along specified dotted lines. These tests just require a little practice and an explanation of how the process works.

When you view the 2-dimensional object the solid lines represent the shape of the pattern and the dashed lines represent fold lines. Attempt to visualize what this shape would look like if the object were folded along the dotted lines. Which of the two shapes does the flat pattern on the left represent, A or B?

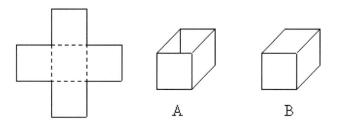

If you fold each part along the dotted lines, you'd recognize that there are only 5 sides that are represented. The top of the box would therefore not be present. "A" would be the proper answer to this question.

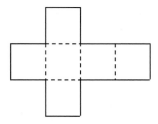

This folding pattern would better represent "B". Most tests will force you to choose between four possible options.

Rounded Shapes

There are many examples in these tests of rounded shapes. You will often see a rounded or curved shape attached to a square, triangle or another object without dotted lines. These objects will not be folded, but may be bent or curved to match the shape of the curved object to which they are attached. For example:

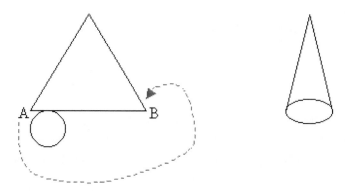

In the above example the triangle is not creased, as point "A" is brought into contact with point "B". The circle is folded over to produce a cone shape as represented on the right. This can also happen with squares, rhombuses, and other objects. The lack of a dotted line indicates that the final shape will not be creased.

General Strategies

1) Observe the Types of Shapes

Many of the questions will become very complex and it may become very difficult to determine which is the correct 3-dimensional picture. Look for matching patterns. For example if there are rounded edges in the 2-dimensional shape, only look at 3-dimensional shapes with similar rounding edges. Eliminate objects with strictly straight edges. For example:

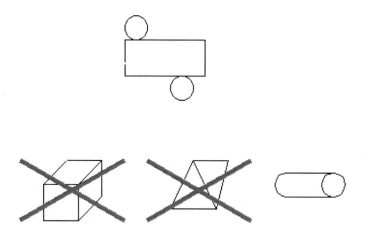

The first two objects are easily eliminated because they lack any round edge.

2) Find a Base

Looking at objects can be overwhelming especially complex ones with multiple folds. One option is to select a base and work from there. Locate that base from your options and work out from there. For example:

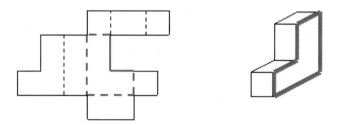

In the above example it would be helpful to pick out a base in the flattened object on the left. The "L" shaped base was selected. Concentrate on that aspect of the pattern, and make your folds from there. The result will be the shape on the right.

3) Eliminate as Many Choices as Possible, then Guess

You are not penalized if you guess incorrectly in these tests. Because there is a time limit, you must be efficient and use your time optimally. Do not waste too much time on one question. Look at your four options, eliminate as many as possible, and then take a guess which of the remaining ones it may be. Remember questions get more difficult throughout the test, so you should expect to spend more time on later questions then earlier ones. The tests are designed to prevent people from answering every possible question. Answer as many correctly as you can.

Spelling Section

The following is a list of words that you should be able to spell.

ability	abundance	absence	absolute
acceleration	acceptable	accessory	accident
accidentally	accuracy	accused	achieved
achievement	acknowledge	acknowledgement	acquaintance
acquired	acquittal	activity	actual
addition	addressed	adequate	administration
admissible	adolescent	advancement	advice
advise	agency	agreement	aggressive
alcohol	alight	align	alleged
allegedly	allergy	alliance	allocate
allowed	alternative	amateur	ambitious
ambulance	analyse	anniversary	announcement
annual	anonymous	answered	anticipated
antique	anxieties	anxious	apologise
apology	appalling	apparent	appeal
appearance	appliance	applicant	argument
artificial	assistance	attachment	authorities
authority	awkward	backwards	balance
bandage	bankrupt	barrister	basis
beautiful	before	behaviour	beneficial
bicycle	blanket	blatant	blockage
blurred	boredom	borrowed	boundaries
breach	broken	breathing	broaden
building	buoyant	bureau	burglaries
calculated	calendar	camera	campaign
candidate	capability	capital	cardboard
career	careful	carriage	casualty
caught	cause	centre	certificate
changing	chaos	character	chemical
circumstances	citizen	civil	claimed
clause	clearance	climate	coincide
colleague	collection	collision	column
combination	comment	commencement	commercial
commission	commissioner	commitment	committee
communication	community	compatible	competent
composure	comprehend	condemned	condition
consequence	consideration	consistent	constant
controversial	controversy	convenient	corpse
corroborate	corruption	coughing	courage
courageous	courteous	cultural	credible
criminal	critical	criticism	crucial
daughter	debris	decentralise	decisive
defendant	demonstrate	denial	deposit

depth	descendant	description	despite
detailed	determined	detour	development
diagnose	diameter	diesel	difference
direction	disability	disappointing	disappointment
disappearance	discipline	discount	discretion
discussion	disguise	dishonest	disillusionment
dismissed	disqualified	distance	distinction
distinguish	distressed	distribute	disturbance
diversity	division	document	domestic
dominant	double	doubtful	draught
duplicate	durable	duration	effective
efficient	electricity	element	eligible
eliminate	embarrass	emergency	eminent
emphasis	employment	empty	encounter
endeavour	energetic	enforce	engagement
enjoyable	enormous	enough	enthusiasm
environment	equality	equation	equipment
equity	eruption	essential	ethnic
evasion	exaggerate	examination	exceed
excess	exception	exceptional	executive
expenses	facilities	fatigue	favourite
feature	February	festival	fictitious
fierce	financial	fixture	floating
flowing	fluorescent	focussed	foreign
foreseeable	forgiveness	formal	fortnight
foundation	fraudulent	frightened	front
fulfilment	function	furniture	gauge
generate	genuine	government	gracious
gradually	grasping	grateful	grievance
grievous	growth	guarantee	guard
guest	guidance	handkerchief	handle
harbour	harden	haste	hazard
headquarters	health	height	heroin
highway	history	holiday	homicide
honesty	honorary	humour	hypnotize
ideal	identification	identify	ignore
illegal	illegible	illusion	illustrate
imagination	imitate	immature	immediately
immensely	immigration	impact	impartial
implement	implication	important	improvement
improvise	impulsive	inaccurate	incapable
incident	inclination	inclusion	income
incorporate	incredible	incriminate	inconsiderate
independent	indicate	indigenous	indirect
individual	industrial	inferior	inflammable

inflation	influence	influential	information
informative	inheritance	initial	initiative
injection	injuries	innocent	inspector
inspiration	instalment	instance	instead
institution	instrument	insulate	insurance
intangible	integrate	integrity	intellectual
intelligent	intend	intensity	intent
intercept	interference	interim	intermittent
internal	interpret	interrupt	view
intrigue	introduction	intrusion	invasion
investigation	invitation	irrational	irreconcilable
irresponsible	irritate	jealous	jeopardy
journalist	joyous	judgement	junior
juror	justice	justification	juvenile
keyboard	kilometre	kitchen	kneel
knocking	knowledge	knowledgeable	known
labourer	lacquer	laminate	language
laundry	lawful	leaflet	league
legality	legible	legislation	legitimate
leisure	length	leverage	liberty
library	licence	licensing	lighten
likelihood	limb	limited	linear
lining	liquidate	liquor	literally
literate	litigation	litre	location
logical	loose	lose	lunged
luxurious	machinery	magazine	magnificent
maintenance	malicious	management	manipulate
mannerism	manslaughter	marijuana	marketing
marriage	masculine	massacre	massive
material	maturity	maximum	mayor
measurement	mechanical	mediate	mediation
medicine	mediocre	memory	merchandise
merge	merit	metropolitan	microscope
middle	military	miniature	minimum
minister	mischievous	misconduct	miserable
missile	mission	mobile	modern
module	momentary	monitored	monopoly
monotonous	monument	motion	mould
mourning	movement	multiply	municipal
murmur	muscle	narcotic	narrative
narrow	nationality	naïve	natural
navigate	nearby	necessary	necessitate
negotiable	negotiation	neighbour	neighbourhood
nervous	neutral	niche	noisy
nominate	normally	nothing	novelty
nudged	nuisance	nurseries	nurture
nutrition	objective	obligation	obscenity
obscure	observation	obstacle	obsolete

obtain	obviously	occasion	occupation
occurred	occurrence	offence	offender
offensive	official	omitted	onus
opening	operation	opinion	opponent
opportunity	opposite	opposition	optimistic
option	ordeal	ordered	ordinary
organisation	orientation	original	otherwise
ought	outcome	outlining	overall
overturn	pacify	paddle	painting
palm	panic	parade	paragraph
parallel	parliament	participate	particle
particularly	particular	partition	partner
passage	patient	patrol	pattern
pause	pavement	payment	peculiar
pedestrian	penalty	pensioner	perceive
percentage	perception	perfect	performance
period	perish	permanent	permissible
permission	persevere	personal	personnel
persuade	pessimistic	petition	petrol
pharmacy	phase	phrase	physical
physique	picture	piece	pivot
placement	plaque	plastic	platform
plead	plenty	plight	plunge
poisonous	policing	policy	political
population	portable	portfolio	portion
position	positive	possession	possibility
postpone	posture	potential	practice
practising	practitioner	praise	precaution
precious	precise	predecessor	prediction
predominantly	preference	preferred	prejudice
preliminary	premature	premium	preparation
prescription	presence	presentation	preserve
pretence	preview	primary	priority
prison	private	privilege	probably
procedure	process	produce	professional
progression	prominent	promise	property
proprietor	prosecution	prospect	protection
protest	proved	provide	provoke
psychological	psychologist	publicity	publish
pulse	puncture	punishment	purchase
purpose	pursue	pursuit	quaint
qualification	qualify	quality	quantify
quantity	quarrelsome	quarter	quash
quell	questionable	queue	quickly
quiet	quite	quotation	racing
radiant	radical	radio	railing
random	range	rapid	rational
rationale	reaching	reactive	reading

realisation	reality	reasonable	reassurance
recalled	recede	receive	reception
recession	recipient	reckless	recognised
recommendation	reconciliation	reconstruct	recovery
recreation	recruit	rectify	recuperate
recurrence	reduction	redundancy	redundant
reference	reflecting	reflex	reformed
refreshment	refrigerator	refusal	registration
rehabilitation	reinforce	rejection	relapse
related	relationship	release	relief
relinquish	remaining	remember	remittance
remote	renowned	repair	repeated
repercussion	repetition	replica	reported
representation	reprisal	research	reservation
residential	resigned	resources	respectable
responsibility	responsible	restaurant	restitution
restriction	resuscitate	retention	retirement
retrenchment	reunited	review	reward
rival	robberies	rogue	rough
ruling	sacrifice	safety	salary
salvage	sample	satellite	savage
savoury	scald	scandal	scarce
schedule	scheme	scholar	scientist
scratched	search	secondary	secretaries
section	security	segment	seized
seizure	selection	sensible	sensitive
sentence	separate	sequence	sergeant
service	session	settlement	several
severe	shrewd	shriek	sign
signal	signature	significant	silence
simultaneous	situation	sizeable	skilful
smear	sociable	society	solemn
solicitor	solution	sophisticated	souvenir
specialize	specific	specifically	specimen
speculate	squander	square	stable
standard	staple	static	stationary
stationery	statistics	statue	strength
subject	submerged	subsequent	subscription
substance	substitute	succeed	sufficient
suggest	superintendent	superior	superstition
supplement	suppose	suppressed	surge
surrendered	survey	susceptible	suspend
suspicion	swallow	sympathy	tactic
technical	telephone	telephonist	syringe
tangled	technological	temperament	tenant
system	target	technology	temperature
tentative	temporary	terminated	termination
terminal	territory	tertiary	terrible

thirsty	thorough	theory	tissue
tobacco	thought	tongue	towards
tomorrow	traffic	tragedy	tradition
transfer	transparent	travelling	transport
triumph	trauma	truthful	turnover
trustworthy	ultimately	unaware	typical
unbelievable	unconscious	unbearable	undertaken
underrate	underground	uniform	union
unforeseen	unnecessary	unreliable	university
vacant	vacation	utilise	valuable
vandalism	vague	vehicle	venture
variation	version	vertical	verge
violence	visible	vigour	vocal
volume	vital	wager	warehouse
volunteer	wastage	waterproof	warrant
western	whereabouts	weapon	wilful
windcheater	whisper	withdrawal	worthy
window	wrong	wrongdoing	writing

Security Requirements

The following are the twelve main components that need to be understood for licencing requirements in Ontario. These same components will be very similar in other provinces across the country.

1) Introduction to the Security Industry

Section Overview
The trainer provides a summary of the principal duties and responsibilities necessary to work effectively in the security industry. Students will learn to interpret and comply with the legal requirements of their occupation as well as identify job roles and responsibilities.

Minimum Requirements
- Describe and compare the different jobs in the security industry (e.g. private investigation, law enforcement, security services, loss prevention, and patrol services)
- Describe the occupation of a security guard with respect to the knowledge, skills, and abilities needed to perform well
- Describe the job specifications, activities, and demands of a security guard (e.g. travel, off-hours, stress, risks, dangers, etc.)

Outline
The trainer provides the student with a background on the security industry including the changes in the industry as a result of the new Private Security and Investigative Services Act, 2005. S/he introduces the student to the challenges and benefits of becoming a security guard. The role of a security guard with respect to the public should be discussed.

2) Private Security and Investigative Services Act and Ministry Code of Conduct

Section Overview
The Private Security and Investigative Services Act, 2005 (PSISA) regulates the security industry. As such, security guards must be familiar with the PSISA to ensure they follow the regulations and prohibitions including the Code of Conduct. The trainer introduces the legislation to the student by outlining all relevant components and explaining the Code of Conduct.

Minimum Requirements
1. Private Security and Investigative Services Act, 2005 (PSISA)
-- Explain an individual's responsibility regarding licensing, including the licensing process and mandatory requirements
-- Describe the general duties, standards, practices, regulations and prohibitions
-- Explain the requirement to produce a licence
2. Code of Conduct
-- Explain the relevant components and the consequences of failing to comply
-- Define complaint procedures

3) Basic Security Procedures

Section Overview

Security guards need to respond to changes in their environment, which includes actions such as traffic movement, ensuring the safety of persons between and within locations, monitoring and managing the access and departure of persons and vehicles and observing and monitoring people. Security guards need to be aware of the correct way to deal with these situations. The trainer provides his/her students with the knowledge and skills to assess the security of physical environments, to apply basic aspects of security in their roles and to assess the impact of drug use in the context of safety for oneself and others.

Minimum Requirements

1. Describe and explain surveillance and address the following surveillance techniques:
- Observing the physical environment
- Attending to environmental details
- Situational awareness

2. Describe the basic elements of security and include the following:
- Access control
- Crowd control
- Vehicle control and legal authority to perform traffic control duties
- Shift handover

3. Discuss drug effects, substance abuse and related drug paraphernalia
- Relate signs of substance abuse and withdrawal including physical and psychological consequences

Note: There are three components in this section: Surveillance, Basic Elements of Security and Drug Effects.

Surveillance Outline

Security guards will be called upon to observe the physical environment for changes and suspicious behaviour. This objective is typically achieved by conducting an in-person or remote surveillance of the physical environment. Security guards are expected to notice and monitor minor changes in order to make sound decisions when devising a plan of action. The trainer focuses on:
-- Decision-making
-- Recognizing patterns (situational awareness)
-- Observing minor, yet critical details
-- Recognizing typicality and detecting anomalies
-- Improvising responses
-- Interpreting and adapting to events
-- Prioritizing actions

Observing and monitoring individuals, identifying and responding to potential threats, different types of patrolling and loss prevention should be discussed.

Basic Elements of Security Outline

Security guards are required to manage individuals, vehicles and materials in a safe and polite manner while assessing a situation for threats and incidents. The trainer addresses the following basic elements of security:

1. Access control
-- How to escort people within and between locations in a safe manner
-- How to prepare for an assignment
-- Contacting the correct personnel when there is a breach of security
-- How to inspect baggage, vehicles, etc. for illegal substances
2. Crowd control
-- How to create a barricade or staging area
-- How to lock down a facility
3. Vehicle control
-- Controlling vehicular/pedestrian traffic on company property or on public roads in emergencies
-- Monitoring traffic movements
-- Using proper hand signals for directing traffic
-- Using traffic control equipment
-- Wearing the appropriate attire
4. Shift handover procedures
-- How to update the next person on shift

Drug Effects Outline

Security guards may encounter individuals under the influence of drugs or alcohol. They need to be aware of the signs of substance abuse as well as the impact of different drugs on human behaviour (e.g. suspect going through withdrawal) in order to deal with these individuals in a manner that will ensure personal safety as well as that of the suspect. The trainer discusses different types of drugs and paraphernalia, the impact of using different drugs on human behaviour and how to address individual behaviour depending on the type of substance abuse.

4) Report Writing

Section Overview

Security guards are required to complete written reports of occurrences, duties performed, and comprehensive descriptions of their tasks/observances. The trainer instructs the student how to write reports that are objective and standardized.

Minimum Requirements

1. Discuss the following elements of report writing:
- How to record relevant factual data and circumstances in a notebook
- The different types and purposes of reports
- Recognizing legal implications of reports and confidentiality
- Incorporating who, what, where, when, why and how in report writing
- How to take a statement
- Identifying the appropriate method of communication to report an issue

Outline

Security guards are required to write a variety of reports for different audiences. It is imperative that reports are written in a clear, standardized format to ensure information is conveyed accurately and without bias. The trainer discusses:
- The importance of using a notebook and the rules and format for taking accurate

notes
- Different types of reports depending on the situation (e.g. incident, use of force, witness statements)
- The basic elements of report writing (e.g. date, time, location, actions/behaviours, description of individuals, observations, time of completion, etc.)
- Content of reports (e.g. factual information only)
- The legal implications of reports (e.g. necessary for audits or evidence in court)
- The difference between statements and reports
- How to properly distribute reports (e.g. problems with e-mailing confidential reports)

5) Health and Safety

Section Overview
The policies and procedures of the Occupational Health and Safety Act and the Workplace Hazardous Materials Information System (WHMIS) are necessary to ensure the occupational safety of security guards and those they interact with. The trainer identifies how to control workplace risks and hazards, how to apply appropriate responses to emergency situations and how to communicate workplace safety requirements.

Minimum Requirements
1. Outline the Occupational Health and Safety Act
2. Outline the Workplace Hazardous Materials Information System (WHMIS)
Outline
The trainer provides a brief introduction to the Occupational Health and Safety Act and Workplace Hazardous Materials Information System (WHMIS). Security guards need to know and understand how the Occupational Health and Safety Act and WHMIS apply to themselves and to others. The trainer should also cover the right to refuse unsafe work.

6) Emergency Response Preparation

Section Overview
Security guards are expected to respond to emergency situations and to minimize the impact caused at a worksite. They may be required to perform a variety of duties during emergency procedures and must understand the importance of scene management. The trainer will address the potential roles of a security guard during an emergency situation and how to effectively complete these tasks.

Minimum Requirements
1. Identify the following criteria of a potential emergency:
-- Risk factors
-- Fire emergencies
-- Bomb emergencies
-- Weapon emergencies
-- Suspicious packages
-- Explosive devices
2. Describe the following emergency response procedures:

-- Explain fire emergency response procedures
-- Explain bomb emergency response procedures
-- Explain weapon emergency response procedures
-- Explain suspicious package emergency response procedures
-- Explain explosive device emergency response procedures
3. Explain the potential roles of a security guard in emergency situations
4. Detail how to implement duty of care
-- Describe legal requirements
-- Detail how to protect and secure a crime scene

Note: There are four components in this section: Emergency Situations, Emergency Response Procedures, Potential Roles of a Security Guard During an Emergency and Duty of Care.

Emergency Situation Outline

Security guards may encounter emergency situations at a worksite. They will need to accurately identify the risk factors associated with fire threats, bomb threats, weapon emergencies, suspicious packages, and explosive devices and learn how to respond appropriately. The trainer outlines the different risk factors a security guard must be familiar with and how to protect individuals and property associated with an assignment (i.e. contain, activate, and evacuate). In addition to emergency responses, the trainer includes an overview of the basic principles of prevention and safety.

Emergency Response Procedures Outline

Security guards must be comfortable when responding to emergency situations, familiar with different emergency procedures and must coordinate these procedures with organizational requirements and/or other personnel. Understanding the need for emergency response procedures and following the emergency response plan for a given site is vital to the security guard role. The trainer provides instruction on the following:
-- The different emergency response procedures (e.g. First Aid and CPR)
-- Common tools associated with response procedures (e.g. fire extinguisher, sprinkler systems)
-- Determining the safest and most appropriate response to a threat
-- How to preserve evidence
-- Proper evacuation protocol and knowledge of access routes
-- How to control access for emergency services and provide necessary details
-- Site-specific building occupant capacity limits (e.g. Ontario Fire Code and building specific regulations with respect to occupancy)

Potential Roles of a Security Guard During an Emergency Outline

Security guards may be required to fulfill different roles during an emergency situation. They may have to assist other personnel (including police, fire, and ambulance) or take the lead in responding to the emergency. Security guards must be able to work alongside other personnel and quickly and accurately understand their role in a given situation. They must recognize when an emergency is beyond the scope of their job specifications and requires additional assistance. The trainer provides an overview of the relationships in the security industry, including a matrix with job titles, descriptions, responsibilities and the link between them to help security guards understand when a situation is beyond their scope and who to contact in specific emergency situations.

Duty of Care Outline

Security guards need to be familiar with the concept of duty of care (what a reasonable person should do in a particular situation) and be capable of securing and protecting a crime scene until the appropriate personnel arrive. The trainer reviews the circumstances that require duty of care and instructs how to secure and protect a crime scene or sentinel event scene.

7) Canadian Legal System

Section Overview

Security guards work within the Canadian Legal System. They need to be familiar with the Criminal Court System, the Ontario Evidence Act, the Canada Evidence Act and how these apply to their positions to ensure the information they obtain is admissible in court. The trainer outlines the difference between criminal, provincial and municipal law as well as case and civil law, the hierarchy of the court system and offences and the requirements for the admissibility of evidence.

Minimum Requirements

1. Discuss the Canadian Criminal Court System
-- Outline the Canadian Criminal Court System, the hierarchy of the court system and court protocols/procedures
-- Describe the protocols and procedures for the purpose of giving evidence
2. Explain commonly accepted approaches to the collection, preservation and presentation of evidence including the handling and sealing of audio/visual materials
3. Explain relevant sections of the Ontario Evidence Act and Canada Evidence Act that pertain to admissible evidence
4. Discuss municipal by-laws

Note: There are three components in this section: Canadian Criminal Court System, Evidence Handling Techniques and Municipal By-laws.

The Ontario Evidence Act and Canada Evidence Act do not specify how evidence is collected, but identify which types of evidence are admissible to the court. The trainer should concentrate on what is considered evidence and which methods a security guard can use to ensure it remains admissible. Security guards are only expected to know the municipal by-laws that relate to their role and where to find this information if it is not readily available on their premises.

Canadian Criminal Court System Outline

Security guards may be required to prepare for legal proceedings, present evidence, prepare themselves and/or witnesses for testimony and follow up on the outcome of court proceedings. Security guards need a general understanding that all investigations should be conducted as if the case could potentially go to trial and therefore handle themselves accordingly to ensure that no procedural or administrative mistakes are made. The trainer covers the skills and knowledge required to present evidence in a judicial environment.

Evidence Handling Techniques Outline

Security guards protect evidence that may be used in court. The trainer will explain how to collect, preserve, and present admissible evidence in court while preventing the evidence from becoming contaminated. Concepts will include an introduction to the process and protocols for handling evidence, including:

-- The proper procedures for collecting and handling audio/video materials
-- The six core steps for containing evidence:

-- Collect	-- Secure
-- Preserve	-- Identify
-- Continuity	-- Log

Municipal By-Laws Outline

Security guards are required to work within the municipal by-laws of their specific location. They need to be familiar with the common by-laws they will encounter in their position (e.g. noise bylaws, occupancy limits, etc.) and where they can locate this information. The trainer focuses on creating awareness that different municipal by-laws exist and need to be considered. It should be noted that the student may obtain/require further training on by-laws relevant to his/her specific position and that the by-laws addressed in this section are the most common to the private security sector.

8) Legal Authorities

Section Overview

The trainer focuses on the broader legal context of private security to instruct the student on his/her rights and limitations when performing duties as a security guard. The trainer will also explain where a security guard derives his/her authority to carry out job functions.

Minimum Requirements

1. List procedures for handling, storing, disseminating and destroying information of a personal nature
2. Address the relevant sections of the Personal Information Protection and Electronic Documents Act (PIPEDA) regarding the protection of personal information
3. Outline the relevant sections of the following legislation:
- Employment Standards Act, 2000
- Labour Relations Act, 1995
- Liquor Licence Act
- Provincial Offences Act
- Residential Tenancies Act, 2006
- Trespass to Property Act
4. Provide the following information with respect to the Criminal Code of Canada:
- Explain the difference between indictable, summary and criminal offences and a security guard's authority to arrest (e.g. citizen's arrest) - List the most common offences encountered by security guards
- Review the sections of the code regarding defense of property and defense of persons

- Explain criminal harassment, mischief, assault, theft, causing disturbances, breaking and entering and possession of stolen property under the code 5. Explain the common elements of tort law in security situations

Note: There are four components in this section: Handling Information and PIPEDA, Additional Legislation, Criminal Code of Canada and Tort Law. Security guards are only expected to be aware of this legislation as it pertains to their roles. The primary focus should be on best practices with respect to acquiring information to resolve security issues in the context of relevant legislation.

Handling Information and PIPEDA Outline
Security guards frequently deal with the collection, storage, dissemination and destruction of information. The trainer discusses the procedures and regulations with respect to managing information and explains how to keep information secure while ensuring that it is maintained in a manner consistent with PIPEDA.

Additional Legislation Outline
Security guards can encounter situations where they need to be familiar with the following legislation:
- Employment Standards Act, 2000
- Labour Relations Act, 1999
- Liquor Licence Act
- Provincial Offences Act
- Residential Tenancies Act, 1996
- Trespass to Property Act

The trainer provides a brief introduction to the relevant sections to each act, addresses the risks and dangers associated with private security and describes how each act can impact the safety and effectiveness on site. Issues of liability should be discussed to ensure the student understands how to complete his/her duties within lawful authority. The trainer also addresses whose authority a security guard is acting on (acting as agent of the property owner) and differences in private versus public property.

Criminal Code of Canada Outline
Security guards may encounter situations in which they need to deal with indictable, summary, or criminal offences. They need to be able to accurately identify and categorize offences when on duty and understand how to perform a citizen's arrest according to the Criminal Code of Canada. The trainer introduces the code within the context of liability, duty of care and lawful authority. Defense of property and defense of persons should also be discussed.

Tort Law Outline
Security guards must ensure that they are completing their job within their lawful authority. The trainer explains the common elements of tort law in security situations.

9) Effective Communications

Section Overview
Security guards encounter a wide range of situations and are required to act

professionally under all circumstances. The trainer reviews the interpersonal and communication skills necessary to adapt to different environments/scenarios and to diffuse situations when required. The importance of using communication to one's advantage should be emphasized.

Minimum Requirements
Communication Skills
1. Discuss the following oral and written communication skills:
- Adjusting a communication style to accommodate an audience or situation
- Using verbal and non-verbal feedback
- Using effective and appropriate language in oral and written communication
- Writing legibly and clearly (e.g. minimal spelling, grammar or typographical errors)
- Effectively communicating main ideas orally and in writing
- Avoiding personal bias/opinion when communicating
- Asking probing questions to obtain information
- Conveying oral information accurately
- Writing accurate reports
2. Explain tactical communication
- Adjusting behaviour/demeanor (e.g. passive vs. aggressive) based on an individual or situation
Interpersonal Skills
3. Discuss the following interpersonal skills:
- Demonstrating sensitivity/empathy to others (e.g. different cultures, persons with disabilities, human rights issues, mental health issues)
- Establishing a rapport with a variety of people for the purpose of building trusting relationships
- Diffusing, avoiding and managing difficult interpersonal relationships and/or potential conflict
- Being assertive yet professional when interacting with the public

Note: There are three components in this section: Communication Skills, Tactical Communication and Interpersonal Skills.

Communication Skills Outline
Security guards must provide clear and concise information. Their position requires them to communicate with a wide array of individuals both orally and in writing and to obtain information from sources that may be unwilling. The trainer addresses active listening, effective writing and note taking.

Tactical Communication Outline
Security guards may need to utilize tactical communication during the course of their assignments. They must maintain their composure and adjust their behaviour to suit the individual and situation. The trainer explains the principles of tactical communication (both verbal and non-verbal, including posture, tone, assertiveness, spatial distance, eye contact, facial expressions) and de-escalation techniques with progressive intervention steps.

Interpersonal Skills Outline

Security guards often interact with a variety of individuals during the course of their duties. Their conduct is vital to the professional image of the security industry as a whole. The trainer describes proper conduct and deportment, how to adapt quickly to different situations and how to perform duties in a culturally appropriate manner. Security guards should be able to scan for potential problems and act in a preventative way to avoid any escalation of events.

10) Sensitivity Training

Section Overview

Security guards often interact with the public on a daily basis. It is important they approach individuals with respect to avoid any biases that may impact how they interrelate with others. The trainer addresses prejudices against ethnic backgrounds, persons with mental or physical disabilities and gender and sexual orientation.

Minimum Requirements

Discuss the following issues:
1. Recognizing one's own biases and describing how these can influence situations
2. Recognizing the impact of mental, physical, cultural and sexual differences on situational dynamics

Outline

Security guards may be required to interact with diverse groups of individuals on a regular basis. The trainer introduces the concept of respect for differences, identifies potential issues that may arise when dealing with a variety of people (e.g. communication difficulties, misinterpretation of gestures) and how to approach individuals in a way that minimizes miscommunication.

11) Use of Force Theory

Section Overview

Security guards may be required to use force during certain situations. The trainer explains use of force theory, the components of the use of force model and how to maintain composure during potentially stressful situations. Students need to attend specialized training to learn how to use defensive equipment and to apply use of force options.

Minimum Requirements

1. Explain the authority to use force under the Criminal Code of Canada
- Discuss the use of force model and its framework components
- Explain how to choose an appropriate use of force component and justify an action
2. Discuss how to act under stress and maintain composure
3. Explain positional asphyxia and excited delirium

Outline

The trainer explains use of force theory based on the National Use of Force Model (modified for security guards) and outlines Section 25 of the Criminal Code of Canada.

Security guards can be put in situations where they need to maintain their professional composure even when under a high level of stress. The trainer will also address how to control a situation by asking questions, dealing with difficult customers/clients/suspects, managing stress when isolated or fatigued and personal health issues such as overall stress levels, stress factors, cleanliness, nutrition, lifestyle and fitness. Positional asphyxia and excited delirium should also be discussed.

12) Emergency Level First Aid

Section Overview
First aid training and certification is a requirement of the basic training program for security guards. An accredited trainer provides instruction that is equivalent to the St. John Ambulance course Emergency Level First Aid.

Minimum Requirements
1. The following topics must be covered:
- Emergency Scene Management
- Shock, Unconsciousness and Fainting
- Choking – Adult
- Severe Bleeding
- One Rescuer CPR – Adult.
2. Training must be delivered by:
- A St. John Ambulance certified instructor, or
- A Workplace Safety and Insurance Board (Ontario) approved first aid trainer

P.I. Requirements

1) Introduction to the Private Investigation Industry
Section Overview
The trainer provides an overview of the principal duties and responsibilities necessary to work effectively in the private investigation industry. The student is introduced to job roles and responsibilities and the different fields of private investigative work.

Minimum Requirements
1. Describe and compare the different jobs in the security industry (e.g. private investigation, law enforcement, security services, loss prevention, and patrol services)
2. Explain the occupational tasks and requirements of a private investigator
- Describe the position of a private investigator with respect to the knowledge, skills and abilities needed to perform well
- Explain the job specifications, activities and demands of a private investigator (e.g., travel, stress, risks, dangers, etc.)
3. Detail the various types of investigations and different specializations of private investigators (e.g. general, legal, insurance, corporate, etc.)

Outline
The trainer provides the student with a background on the private investigation industry

including the new standardization and regulation of the field. S/he introduces the student to the challenges and benefits of becoming a private investigator.

2) The Private Security and Investigative Services Act
Section Overview
The Private Security and Investigative Services Act, 2005 (PSISA) regulates the private investigation industry. As such, private investigators must be familiar with the PSISA to ensure they follow the regulations and prohibitions. The trainer introduces the legislation to the student by outlining all relevant components.

Minimum Requirements
1. Private Security and Investigative Services Act, 2005 (PSISA)
- Explain an individual's responsibility regarding licensing, including the licensing process and mandatory requirements
- Describe the general duties, standards, practices, regulations and prohibitions
- Explain the requirement to produce a licence
2. Code of Conduct
- Introduce the regulation and the consequences of failing to comply
- Define complaint procedures

Outline
This section introduces the student to his/her responsibilities as a private investigator under the PSISA. The trainer provides instruction on all the relevant requirements of the PSISA, the consequences for non-compliance and public complaint procedures. The authority to conduct investigations and surveillance should also be discussed.

3) Provincial and Federal Statutes
Section Overview
The student is introduced to the various statutes that apply to the field of private investigation in Ontario. The trainer addresses how criminal, civil, case and common law vary and explains the difference between provincial and federal statutes. It should be noted that the student may obtain/require further training on statutes that are relevant to his/her specific position and that the legislation addressed in this section is the most common to the private investigation sector.

Minimum Requirements
1. Discuss the relevant sections of the Personal Information Protection and Electronic Documents Act (PIPEDA), Freedom of Information and Protection of Privacy Act (FIPPA), and the Municipal Freedom of Information and Protection of Privacy Act (MFIPPA) that apply to the handling of information and the ability to access government information
2. Introduce the Ontario Evidence Act and Canada Evidence Act in relation to the admissibility/inadmissibility of evidence and who is eligible to give evidence
3. Outline the relevant sections of the following legislation:
- Employment Standards Act, 2000
- Occupational Health and Safety Act
- Labour Relations Act, 1995
- Provincial Offences Act

- Residential Tenancies Act, 2006
- Trespass to Property Act

Note: This section has three components: Handling Information and PIPEDA / FIPPA / MFIPPA, Ontario Evidence Act and Canada Evidence Act and Additional Legislation. Private investigators are only expected to be aware of this legislation as it pertains to their roles. The primary focus should be on best practices with respect to acquiring information in the context of relevant legislation.

Handling Information and PIPEDA / FIPPA / MFIPPA Outline
Private investigators frequently deal with the collection, storage, dissemination and destruction of highly sensitive information. The trainer explains the procedures and regulations with respect to accessing and managing this kind of information. The student should learn how to obtain government information according to the freedom of information laws that regulate the different levels of government.

Ontario Evidence Act and Canada Evidence Act Outline
Private investigators will be called upon to present evidence in court. The trainer outlines the relevant sections of the Ontario Evidence Act and Canada Evidence Act, explaining how these statutes apply to the role of a private investigator. The student must learn the importance of documenting and preserving evidence and understand evidentiary concerns (e.g. acquiring pertinent information or when to stop an investigation). Note: The Ontario Evidence Act and Canada Evidence Act do not specify how evidence is collected, but identify which types of evidence are admissible to the court. The trainer should concentrate on what is considered evidence and which methods a private investigator can use to ensure it remains admissible. The application of the Ontario Evidence Act and Canada Evidence Act in relation to the processing and managing of admissible evidence will be addressed in Section 5: Investigative Techniques.

Additional Legislation Outline
Private investigators can encounter situations where they need to be familiar with additional legislation, especially when undercover. The trainer provides a brief introduction to the relevant sections to each of the following legislation:
- Employment Standards Act, 2000
- Occupational Health and Safety Act
- Labour Relations Act, 1995
- Provincial Offences Act
- Residential Tenancies Act, 2006
- Trespass to Property Act

The trainer addresses the risks and dangers associated with private investigation and describes how each act can impact the safety and effectiveness of conducting investigations. Issues of liability should be discussed to ensure the student understands how to complete an investigation within lawful authority.

4) Criminal and Civil Law
Section Overview
Private investigators are expected to work in accordance with a wide range of criminal

and civil legislative and procedural requirements while balancing their own organizational requirements. The trainer outlines the key legal and procedural principles of criminal and civil law as it applies to private investigation.

Minimum Requirements
Level of Authority
1. Explain the authority to arrest under the Criminal Code of Canada
- Describe the difference between a citizen's authority to arrest and a police officer's
- Detail what a private investigator would have to present to the police to have an arrest made
2. Discuss the different criminal offences
- Explain what constitutes an indictable offence under the Criminal Code of Canada
- Explain what constitutes an offence punishable on summary conviction under the Criminal Code of Canada
- Explain the concept of private information in relation to a private investigator charging an individual with an offence
3. Outline the Canadian Criminal Court System
- Discuss the Canadian Criminal Court System, hierarchy of the court system and court protocols/procedures
- Explain court protocols and procedures for the purpose of giving evidence
4. Describe what constitutes intimidation under the Criminal Code of Canada and the effects of intimidation and stalking when conducting surveillance
5. Explain the common elements of tort law and address libel, slander and perjury

Note: This section has five components: Criminal Code of Canada, Criminal Offences, Canadian Criminal Court System, Intimidation and Tort Law, Libel, Slander and Perjury.

Criminal Code of Canada Outline
The trainer provides an overview of the Criminal Code of Canada, including a breakdown of the different parts and a segment on how to read law. Section 2 of the code should be addressed with particular reference to the definition of a peace officer and a public officer. The student must also be instructed on Section 494 and how to perform a citizen's arrest.

Criminal Offences Outline
Private investigators may encounter situations involving indictable or summary offences under the Criminal Code of Canada. They need to be able to accurately identify and categorize these offences when on duty. The trainer provides an introduction to the different types of offences and the common offences that must be known to make a citizen's arrest.

Canadian Criminal Court System Outline
environment. Private investigators may be required to prepare for legal proceedings, present evidence and follow up on the outcomes. Every investigation should be conducted as if the case could potentially go to trial and procedural and administrative requirements should be completed with the utmost care. The trainer discusses the different levels of the court system including how to prepare for trial/court, how to prepare for testimony, how to share the results of an investigation or evidence and how to

prepare witnesses for court.

Intimidation Outline

Private investigators may be put in situations where intimidation, as defined by the Criminal Code of Canada, occurs. They must be able to recognize when intimidation is being used against them and how they can become involved in intimidation and/or stalking when conducting surveillance. The trainer explains the consequences of breaching the Criminal Code of Canada and how intimidation and stalking may impact the admissibility of evidence. Section 423 of the code is discussed.

Tort Law, Libel, Slander and Perjury Outline

Private investigators must ensure that they are completing their job within their lawful authority. The trainer explains the common/relevant elements of tort law, libel, slander and perjury that are required to investigate the facts of a case appropriately.

5) Investigative Techniques
Section Overview

Private Investigators often encounter a multitude of different situations on a regular basis. They need to have a thorough knowledge of research techniques, surveillance techniques, interviewing techniques, industry specific equipment and how to collect and preserve evidence. It is also imperative that private investigators understand how to take proper and complete notes. The trainer details the techniques and skills required to conduct investigations.

Minimum Requirements

1. Explain commonly accepted approaches for the following:
- Collecting, preserving and presenting evidence
- Storing, disseminating and destroying information of a personal nature
- Handling and sealing audio/visual materials
2. List the relevant sections of the Evidence Act and Canada Evidence Act that pertain to admissible evidence
3. Describe the sequential steps of an investigation and different investigative methods
4. Explain the following research techniques:
- How to access public/proprietary sources of information (e.g. industry-related databases)
- How to access industry-specific information
- The basic techniques used to gather information on people, places or things
5. Describe the different types of surveillance and address the following surveillance techniques:
- Observing the physical environment
- Attending to environmental details
- Situational awareness
- Identifying unusual behaviour/situations/activities
- Maintaining awareness/vigilance of surroundings
- Choosing an optimal location for surveillance
- Drawing on knowledge and experience to focus observations
- Recording appropriate/relevant details and ensuring accuracy of information
- Consistently re-evaluating the situation

6. Explain standard interview techniques and discuss the following:
- How to conduct an interview in an arrest situation and in a non-arrest situation
7. Provide instruction on the proper use of industry related equipment
8. Provide instruction on how to write a report

Note: This section has eight components: Handling and Sealing Audio/Video Materials, Ontario Evidence Act and Canada Evidence Act, Conducting Investigations, Research Techniques, Principles of Surveillance, Interview Techniques, Using Industry Related Equipment and Report Writing.

Handling and Sealing Audio/Video Materials Outline

Private investigators often need to handle and seal audio and video materials from investigations. The trainer outlines the proper hands-on procedures for dealing with these materials to ensure their admissibility in court. Concepts will include an introduction to the process and protocols for handling evidence, including:
- Collecting, preserving and presenting evidence
- Inventory control and evidence chain of custody
- The six core steps for containing evidence:
- Collect   - Secure   - Preserve
- Identify   - Continuity   - Log

Storing, disseminating and destroying information of a personal nature should be addressed.

Ontario Evidence Act and Canada Evidence Act Outline

Private investigators protect evidence and appear in court as witnesses. The trainer instructs the student how to collect, preserve, and present admissible evidence in court while avoiding contaminating the evidence. Reading material from Section 3 should be reviewed and there should be a focus on the six key steps for processing and managing admissible evidence (collect, secure, preserve, identify, continuity and log).

Conducting Investigations Outline

The primary responsibility of a private investigator is to conduct investigations and it is vital that the student learn the proper techniques to be successful in the occupation. The trainer provides an introduction to the fundamentals of investigation and addresses preliminary, detailed and follow-up investigations. Trainers should refer to the various types of investigations (e.g. corporate espionage, workplace theft, insurance fraud, etc.) while discussing techniques.

Research Techniques Outline

Private investigators must be capable of conducting research to assist their investigations. The trainer explains fundamental research techniques including how to conduct a full background/due diligence check and how to cross-reference. Available sources of information and research tools should be discussed (e.g. internet, databases, archival data, etc.).

Principles of Surveillance Outline

Private investigators must be capable of conducting surveillance and are required to understand the legislation governing criminal harassment and intimidation as these offences relate to surveillance operations. Reading material from Section 4 should be reviewed and the following fundamentals of surveillance should be introduced:

- Methods of surveillance
- Mobile/stationary
- Strategic positioning - distance, pacing, location
- Preparation work - content of vehicle, site surveillance/scouting, scheduling, etc.
- Cross-reference note taking, surveillance data, and reports (matching process)
- Best practices
- Situational awareness guidelines for assessing, recognizing and recalling investigations
- Overt/covert
- Surveillance techniques

Interview Techniques Outline

Private investigators are required to interview individuals in order to obtain information for their assignments. The trainer provides an introduction to fundamental interview techniques and addresses the following:

- The difference between interviewing and interrogating
- Different types of interviews
- Narrative versus cognitive interviews
- Civil versus criminal interviews
- Note taking procedures
- The protocols for statement taking and the law in relation to statements
- Utilizing other resources (statement analysis, profiling)
- Communication theory
- How to assess the credibility, reliability and suitability of a witness

Using Industry Related Equipment Outline

The trainer discusses how to select and operate necessary occupational equipment for different situations. The student is introduced to the basic technical knowledge needed to efficiently use the equipment and routine maintenance should be addressed. The following tools are discussed:

- Tape recorder
- Camera
- Day/night goggles
- Tripod
- Video camera - overt/covert
- Dictation recorder
- Binoculars

Report Writing Outline

Private investigators regularly complete written reports of occurrences, duties performed and comprehensive descriptions of their tasks/observances. They need to create reports that are objective and standardized. The student is introduced to different types of situational reports (e.g. legal or insurance) as well as basic report writing protocols such as: date, time, location, actions/behaviours, description of individuals, observations, time of completion, etc. In addition, the trainer explains the legal implications of reports (e.g. for auditing or evidence purposes).

6) Principles of Ethical Reasoning/Decision-Making
Section Overview

Private Investigators are required to make quick decisions in a variety of situations and must utilize good judgment. They need to recognize and appropriately handle ethical dilemmas relating to diversity, cultural differences and contemporary social problems. The trainer discusses the PSISA Code of Conduct and the concept of duty of care.

Minimum Requirements
1. Discuss relevant components of the Code of Conduct and explain the meaning of duty of care
2. Outline the following principles of decision-making:
- Recognizing differences between relevant/irrelevant facts and details
- Making sound and defensible decisions supported by facts and research
- Making appropriate judgments suited to the time-frame, risks and facts of the case and potential hazards/dangers in the situation
- Prioritizing situations/decisions/tasks
- Drawing on legislation and laws to make decisions
- Preparing next logical steps required for a task/job
- Determining who should/should not have access to sensitive or confidential information/locations/people (PIPEDA)
- Recognizing ethical dilemmas
- Recognizing issues relating to diversity, cultural differences and contemporary social problems (e.g. stereotyping and discrimination)

Note: There are two components in this section: Code of Conduct and Duty of Care and Decision-Making.

Code of Conduct and Duty of Care Outline
Private investigators need to be familiar with the Code of Conduct and the concept of duty of care, which outlines what a reasonable person should do in a particular situation. The trainer reviews the circumstances that require duty of care.

Decision-Making Outline
Private investigators are required to make quick and ethical decisions and need to deal with issues of discrimination and prejudice in an unbiased manner. The trainer provides the student with an introduction to ethical reasoning and decision-making and addresses the following:
- The theory of ethical reasoning and decision-making
- Recognizing patterns (situational awareness)
- Recognizing typicality and detecting anomalies
- The effects and consequences of discrimination, prejudice and stereotyping Issues such as impartiality, conflict of interest, entrapment and other scenarios that require effective decision-making should be discussed.

7) Key Principles of Communication and Interaction
Section Overview
Private Investigators encounter a wide range of situations and are required to act professionally under all circumstances. The trainer reviews the interpersonal and communication skills necessary to adapt to different environments/scenarios and to diffuse situations when required. The importance of using communication to one's advantage should be emphasized.

Minimum Requirements
Communication Skills
1. Discuss the following oral and written communication skills:
- Adjusting a communication style to accommodate an audience or situation
- Using verbal and non-verbal feedback
- Using effective and appropriate language in oral and written communication
- Writing legibly and clearly (e.g. minimal spelling, grammar or typographical errors)
- Effectively communicating main ideas orally and in writing
- Avoiding personal bias/opinion when communicating
- Asking probing questions to obtain information
- Conveying oral information accurately
2. Explain tactical communication
- Adjusting behaviour/demeanor (e.g. passive vs. aggressive) based on an individual or situation
Interpersonal Skills
3. Discuss the following interpersonal skills:
- Demonstrating sensitivity/empathy to others (e.g. different cultures, persons with disabilities, human rights issues, mental health issues)
- Establishing a rapport with a variety of people for the purpose of building trusting relationships
- Diffusing, avoiding and managing difficult interpersonal relationships and/or potential conflict
- Being assertive yet professional when interacting with the public

Note: There are three components in this section: Communication Skills, Tactical Communication, and Interpersonal Skills.

Communication Skills Outline
Private Investigators must provide clear and concise information. Their position requires them to communicate with a wide array of individuals both orally and in writing and to obtain information from sources that may be unwilling. The trainer addresses active listening, effective writing techniques and note taking.

Tactical Communication Outline
Private Investigators may need to utilize tactical communication during the course of their assignments. They must maintain their composure and adjust their behaviour to suit the individual and situation. The trainer explains the principles of tactical communication (both verbal and non-verbal, including posture, tone, assertiveness, spatial distance, eye contact, facial expressions) and de-escalation techniques with progressive intervention steps.

Interpersonal Skills Outline
Private Investigators often interact with a variety of individuals during the course of their duties. Their conduct is vital to the professional image of the security industry as a whole. The trainer describes proper conduct and deportment, how to adapt quickly to different situations and how to perform duties in a culturally appropriate manner. Private Investigators should be able to scan for potential problems and act in a preventative way to avoid any escalation of events.

8) Self-Management Skills
Section Overview
The trainer discusses the skills and knowledge required to work individually and as part of a team. Private investigators must be able to assess their own roles and responsibilities within a larger team framework, use acquired interpersonal skills to build positive relationships and comply with legislative and procedural requirements to complete tasks within designated timeframes.

Minimum Requirements
1. Discuss how to act under stress while maintaining professional composure
2. Address the following time management skills:
- Multitasking in a quick and efficient manner
- Completing tasks within allotted timeframes
- Prioritizing time to complete tasks safely and effectively
- Arriving to assignments on time
3. Discuss the ability to work independently and in a team and address the following:
- Working well with others to accomplish mutual objectives
- Understanding conditions/situations that are best accomplished by working in a team
- Understanding the strengths and weaknesses of team members, drawing on talents and compensating accordingly
4. Explain flexibility/adaptability requirements in the workplace:
- Being prepared for any type of investigation
- Ability to modify actions, appearance or image to changing circumstances and environment
- Adjusting to demands and changes in schedule, location, work environments, weather, and priorities
- Adjusting to clients' needs, preferences, and requirements
- Working in physically or personally uncomfortable environments
- Creating distinct and convincing presences/personae across different assignments

Note: There are four components in this section: Acting Under Stress, Time Management, Working Independently and in a Team and Adaptability.

Acting Under Stress Outline
Private investigators can encounter high-stress situations and must maintain their professional composure. The trainer will explain what to do if exposed when conducting surveillance, how to control situations by asking questions and when one should identify oneself. The trainer will also address how to manage stress when dealing with isolation, driving, and fatigue.

Time Management Outline
Private investigators work under stringent timelines. The trainer discusses how to prioritize multiple tasks at once including how to properly manage cases, time, different types of reports and dealing with shift work.

Working Independently and in a Team Outline
Private investigators may be assigned to situations where they need to work in isolation or within a team. They need to be able to work under a variety of circumstances and be

able to understand the different working styles of colleagues (e.g. two person surveillance, inter-agency cooperation).

Adaptability Outline
Private investigators can encounter a multitude of situations and must adjust to changes quickly while maintaining their composure. The trainer will discuss how to prepare for a variety of situations and how to adjust to work environment and demands (e.g. sitting for long periods, in stairwells, confined environments, etc.).

GCT Level 2

The General Competency Test: Level 2 (GCT2) measures an individual's general cognitive ability. There are 90 multiple-choice questions. The categories of the exam include:

· Vocabulary
· Figural Relations
· Number and Letter Series
· Numerical Problems
· Analytical Reasoning

The test takes 2 1/4 hours to write and the minimum pass mark is 51/90. If you are unsuccessful you must wait 180 days before you can rewrite the test.

Only paper, pencils, erasers and calculators are allowed - no books, dictionaries, notes, or other aids are permitted in the room.

Detach the answer key to take the test.

	A B C D			A B C D E F G H			A B C D	
1)	○○○○	____	11)	○○○○ ○○○○	____	21)	○○○○	____
2)	○○○○	____	12)	○○○○ ○○○○	____	22)	○○○○	____
3)	○○○○	____	13)	○○○○ ○○○○	____	23)	○○○○	____
4)	○○○○	____	14)	○○○○ ○○○○	____	24)	○○○○	____
5)	○○○○	____	15)	○○○○ ○○○○	____	25)	○○○○	____
6)	○○○○	____	16)	○○○○ ○○○○	____	26)	○○○○	____
7)	○○○○	____	17)	○○○○ ○○○○	____	27)	○○○○	____
8)	○○○○	____	18)	○○○○ ○○○○	____	28)	○○○○	____
9)	○○○○	____	19)	○○○○ ○○○○	____	29)	○○○○	____
10)	○○○○	____	20)	○○○○ ○○○○	____	30)	○○○○	____

	A B C D			A B C D			A B C D	
31)	○○○○	____	41)	○○○○	____	51)	○○○○	____
32)	○○○○	____	42)	○○○○	____	52)	○○○○	____
33)	○○○○	____	43)	○○○○	____	53)	○○○○	____
34)	○○○○	____	44)	○○○○	____	54)	○○○○	____
35)	○○○○	____	45)	○○○○	____	55)	○○○○	____
36)	○○○○	____	46)	○○○○	____	56)	○○○○	____
37)	○○○○	____	47)	○○○○	____	57)	○○○○	____
38)	○○○○	____	48)	○○○○	____	58)	○○○○	____
39)	○○○○	____	49)	○○○○	____	59)	○○○○	____
40)	○○○○	____	50)	○○○○	____	60)	○○○○	____

	A B C D	E F G H			A B C D			A B C D	
61)	○○○○		____	71)	○○○○	____	81)	○○○○	____
62)	○○○○		____	72)	○○○○	____	82)	○○○○	____
63)	○○○○		____	73)	○○○○	____	83)	○○○○	____
64)	○○○○	○○○○	____	74)	○○○○	____	84)	○○○○	____
65)	○○○○	○○○○	____	75)	○○○○	____	85)	○○○○	____
66)	○○○○	____		76)	○○○○	____	86)	○○○○	____
67)	○○○○	____		77)	○○○○	____	87)	○○○○	____
68)	○○○○	____		78)	○○○○	____	88)	○○○○	____
69)	○○○○	____		79)	○○○○	____	89)	○○○○	____
70)	○○○○	____		80)	○○○○	____	90)	○○○○	____

Question 1

The neighbourhood children are waiting for the bus. They are in kindergarten, grade 2, 3, 6, 7 and 9. Lisa is in a lower grade than Bonnie, but in a higher grade than Jimmy. Michael is in the lowest grade. Robert is in a grade lower than Jimmy. Bonnie is two grades lower than Rachael. Robert is older than Michael but younger than Jimmy. Rachael is oldest of all. Jimmy is three grades higher than Michael. What grade is Bonnie in?

a) 7th — a) 7th

b) 6th

c) 3rd

d) 9th

Question 2

The horse race is underway. The solid brown horse is ahead of the solid black horse, who is ahead of the white horse with black spots. The black horse with brown spots is trailing the white horse with brown spots. Which horse is in second place?

a) White with brown spots.

b) Solid brown.

c) Black with brown spots.

d) Solid black.

Question 3

Three girls on the gymnastics team recently completed a competition. Their events were beam, bars and floor. Amber placed second in beam, ahead of Elaine. Sarah was last on the bars, immediately behind Elaine. The team member who placed 2nd and 3rd in the other two events placed 1st in floor. What place did Sarah get on the beam?

a) 3rd

b) 2nd

c) 1st

d) 4th

Question 4

There are more employees working at noon than overnight. There are fewer employees working in the morning than in the evening. Morning and evening times require more employees than noon and overnight. Which shift uses the most employees?

a) Morning.

b) Evening.

c) Noon.

d) Overnight.

Question 5

Four women are talking about their favourite flower. They agree on Indian paintbrush, bluebonnet, daisy and rose. Each chooses a different favourite. Roberta likes the flower whose colour starts with the letter of her first name. Nancy's favourite colour is blue and so is her flower. Veronica does not like the Indian paintbrush. What is Tina's favourite flower?

a) Daisy.

b) Rose.

c) Indian paintbrush.

d) Bluebonnet.

Question 6

Students trying out for the swim team are tested to see how far they can swim. Gina has an asthma attack while in the water and has to stop swimming. Tina swims 10 metres less than Nina and 45 metres less than Christa. Who was able to swim the farthest?

a) Christa.   b) Tina.
c) Gina.   d) Nina.

Question 7

The men in an office decided to measure how much water they were drinking in a day. Ryan was drinking more than Tom. Jim was drinking less than Tom and Bob was drinking less than Jim. Who was drinking the second least amount of water each day?

a) Ryan.   b) Jim.
c) Bob.   d) Tom.

Question 8

The women in an office compared the different lengths of their hair. Britney has longer hair than Veronica, but shorter hair than Courtney. Lisa and Veronica have the same length of hair. Suzanne has longer hair than Julie. Julie has the same length of hair as Britney. Who in the office has medium-length hair?

a) Courtney and Lisa.   b) Julie and Lisa.
c) Veronica and Suzanne.   d) Britney and Julie.

Question 9

Some friends go to adopt a cat at the local pet store. There is an orange tabby, a white, long haired Persian, a tan Siamese with blue eyes and a calico mix. Julie does not like the colour white and is allergic to long fur. Charlie only likes long-haired cats and does not like cats with blue eyes. Leslie only likes blue-eyed cats and Danny does not mind a mixed cat. Julie's favourite color is orange. What cat does Charlie pick?

a) White Persian.   b) Tan Siamese.
c) Orange tabby.   d) Calico mix.

Question 10

The rehabilitation clinic sees more knee than neck problems. They see more shoulder problems than back problems. They see fewer shoulder problems than neck problems, but more knee than neck problems. What is the problem most often seen at the rehabilitation clinic?

a) Shoulder.   b) Neck.
c) Knee.   d) Back.

Question 11

Which is the missing image in the following patterns?

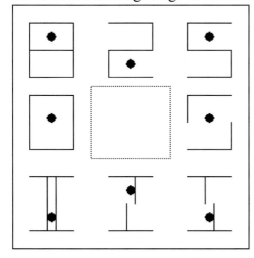

a)

b)

c)

d)

e)

f)

g)

h)

Question 12

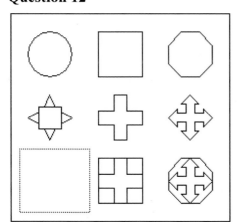

a)

b)

c)

d)

e)

f)

g)

h)

Question 13

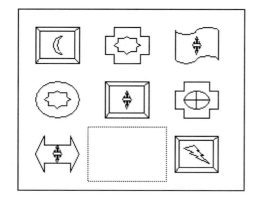

a)

b)

c)

d)

e)

f)

g)

h)

Question 14

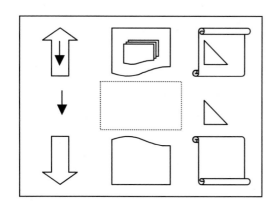

a)

b)

c)

d)

e)

f)

g)

h)

Question 15

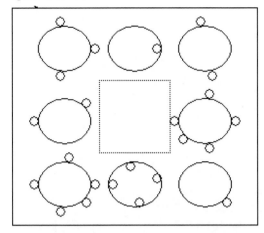

 a)

 b)

 c)

 d)

 e)

 f)

 g)

 h)

Question 16

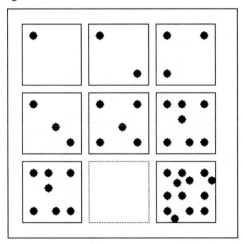

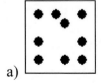 a)

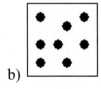 b)

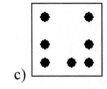 c)

 d)

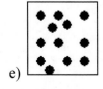 e)

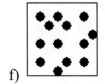 f)

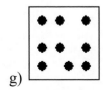 g)

 h)

Question 17

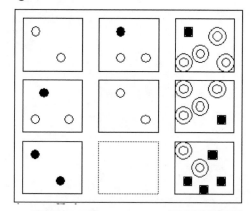

a)   b)   c)   d)

e)   f)   g)   h)

Question 18

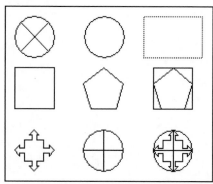

a)   b)   c)   d)

e)   f)   g)   h)

Question 19

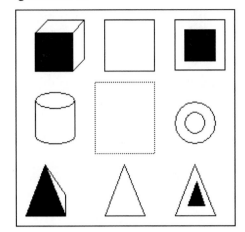

a)

b)

c)

d)

e)

f)

g)

h)

Question 20

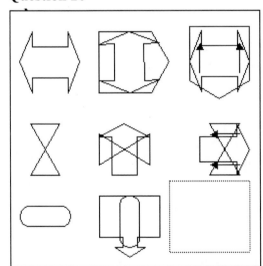

a)

b)

c)

d)

e)

f)

g)

h)

Question 21

75 people came to the single's dance. If there were five more women than men, how many men were there?

a) 25

b) 30

c) 35

d) none of these

Question 22

Paulina is painting a picture on a canvas measuring 2 m by 3 m. She has painted 35% of the area. How much area is left to be painted?

a) 2.7 meters squared

b) 3.5 meters squared

c) 3.9 meters squared

d) 4.3 meters squared

Question 23

Natasha Kaya works 8 hours a day, 38 hours a week. She earns $6 an hour. How much will she earn in 3 weeks?

a) $226

b) $228

c) $660

d) $684

Question 24

A car stereo was stolen from a car outside of the pawn shop. It was originally purchased for $600. Street value is only 15% of the original purchase price. How much can the criminal resell the stereo for?

a) $15

b) $65

c) $70

d) $90

Question 25

140 pounds of drugs are confiscated during an arrest. There is marijuana, cocaine and crystal meth. If 20% of the drugs are cocaine and the remainder was made up of equal parts of marijuana and crystal meth, how many pounds of marijuana were confiscated?

a) 42 pounds

b) 50 pounds

c) 56 pounds

d) 62 pounds

Question 26

In phys. Ed class, Stephen Chan completed the 4 km run in 24 minutes. What is this speed in kilometres per hour?

a) 10

b) 11

c) 12

d) 13

Question 27

Solve for "x": $(7 - x) / 4 = x - 10$

a) 11.3

b) 9.4

c) 7.4

d) 5.3

Question 28

A sink holds 12 L of water. Water drains from it at a rate of 44 L a minute. How long would it take to empty the sink?

a) 1.2 minutes   b) 16 seconds

c) 12 seconds   d) 20 seconds

Question 29

Water flows through a pipe at 20,000 cm cubed per second. How many minutes does it take to fill a rectangular tank 3m x 4m x 5m?

a) 20 minutes   b) 35 minutes

c) 50 minutes   d) none of these

Question 30

There are 240 people at a picnic. People have a choice of cola or lemonade. For every two people that had a cola, one had a lemonade. How many people had cola?

a) 100   b) 160

c) 190   d) none of these

Question 31

If, when driving, you see a ball bounce into the road you should look for a _____ to come next.

a) bat   b) car

c) child   d) bicycle

Question 32

The young prince was so _____ , he laid his coat over a puddle for the princess to step over.

a) gallant   b) inhibited

c) passive   d) timid

Question 33

In the Middle Ages _____ were used to throw large stones over fortified walls.

a) pistols   b) catapults

c) shotguns   d) slingshots

Question 34

A country which does not take sides during a war or international crises is considered to be _____.

a) neutral   b) aggressive

c) threatening   d) chicken

Question 35

When an aquatic rescue is being made, Coast Guard officers need to avoid placing too much _____ on the rescue lines. This can cause the lines to snap.

a) laxity

b) strain

c) water

d) lubricant

Question 36

Identify the synonym for the following words.

Prototype

a) Archetype

b) Typewriter Ribbon

c) Standard

d) Oblique

Question 37

Arbitration

a) Severance

b) Mediation

c) Aggression

d) Channel

Question 38

Council

a) Advice

b) Judgment

c) Ruling Body

d) Encourage

Question 39

Revere

a) Turn Around

b) Despise

c) Respect

d) Coat Lapel

Question 40

Route

a) Intercourse

b) Direction

c) Challenge

d) Encourage

Question 41

Identify which number should replace the asterisk in the following questions.

	135	486
36	45	162
*	15	27

a) 6

b) 8

c) 10

d) None of the above.

Question 42

	203	207
195	197	199
189	191	*

a) 196   b) 193

c) 197   d) None of the above.

Question 43

12	48	*
6		96
3	12	48

a) 154   b) 176

c) 192   d) None of the above.

Question 44

4	12	72
2	6	*
1		18

a) 30   b) 36

c) 22   d) None of the above.

Question 45

103	354	*
225	476	727
	351	602

a) 601   b) 724

c) 607   d) None of the above.

Question 46

What are the missing numbers in the following patterns?
?, 16, 32, 64, 128, 256, ?...

a) 10, 524   b) 8, 512

c) 6, 412   d) None of the above.

Question 47

-14, ?, ?, 7, 14, 21...

a) -7, -1   b) -6, -1

c) -7, 0   d) None of the above.

Question 48

100, 97, 91, 82, 70, ?...

a) 61

b) 65

c) 67

d) None of the above.

Question 49

2, 8, 26, 80, ?...

a) 240

b) 232

c) 252

d) None of the above.

Question 50

?, 15, 27, 51, ?, 195...

a) 9, 93

b) 7, 97

c) 9, 99

d) None of the above.

Question 51

You are expecting an important shipment of auto parts. You placed the order three weeks ago, but the suppliers advised it would be running late. Four days ago you were advised that the parts were arriving in six days, and would immediately be shipped to you. You typically expect shipping to take two days. When should you expect the delivery?

a) 4 days

b) 2 weeks

c) 8 days

d) 10 days

Question 52

The ladies in the office wear different styles of pants and skirts. There are fewer long skirts than short skirts. There are fewer shorts than long skirts. There are more shorts than pants. Which type of clothing is the least prevalent in the office?

a) Short skirts.

b) Pants.

c) Long skirts.

d) Shorts.

Question 53

Four teams are playing in a tournament. Half way through the day, Team 4 is ahead of Team 1, but behind Team 2. Team 3 is ahead of Team 2 at this point in the day. Which team is in the same place as their team number?

a) Team 1.

b) Team 2.

c) Team 3.

d) Team 4.

Question 54

The family has decided to paint four rooms in the house: the kitchen, the dining room, the master bedroom and the guest bathroom. The kitchen is larger than the guest bathroom, but smaller than the dining room. The master bedroom is not smaller than any of the rooms. Which room will take the least amount of paint?

a) Dining room.   b) Master bedroom.

c) Kitchen.   d) Guest bathroom.

Question 55

The customer service department determines bonuses paid based on the number of calls an employee completes each day. Kristina handles twice as many calls as Frank. Frank handles more calls than Natalie. Angela handles as many as Natalie and Frank combined. Which operator handles the most calls?

a) Frank.   b) Angela.

c) Natalie.   d) Kristina.

Question 56

What are the next items in the patterns below?

a)

b)

c)

d)

Question 57

Apple, cat, enigma, giraffe…

a) Ostrich, umbrella, guinea   b) Insane, kitten, monkey

c) Stop, under, yak   d) Cantaloupe, quill, wombat

Question 58

Apple, car, bat, dingo, cover, engine…

a) Oat, nickel, simple, rhinoceros

b) Elephant, jungle, tipped, car

c) Dent, fox, elbow, goose

d) Quail, walrus, x-ray, zebra

Question 59

a)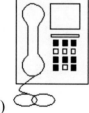

b)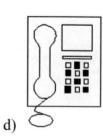

c)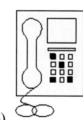

d)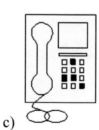

Question 60

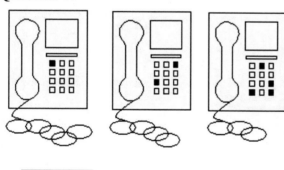

a)

b)

c)

d)

Question 61

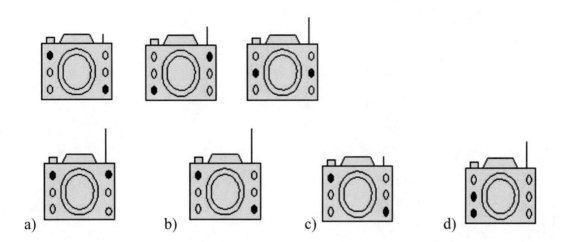

a)   b)   c)   d)

Question 62

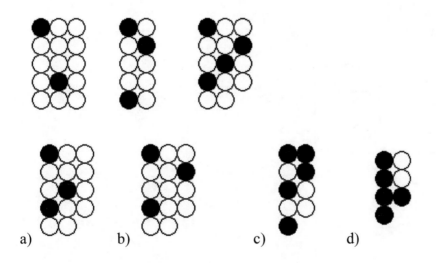

a)   b)   c)   d)

Question 63

AB YZ CD WX EF ...

a) OP GH KL ST   b) UV JK NO AB
c) UV GH OP IJ   d) QR KL MN ST

Question 64

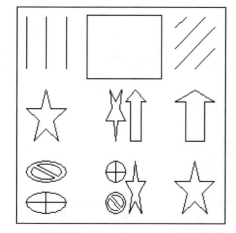

a)   b)   c)   d)

e)   f)   g)   h)

Question 65

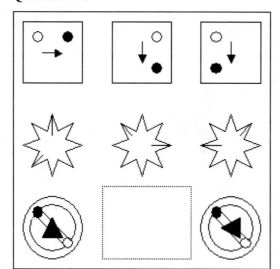

a)   b)   c)   d)

e)   f)   g)   h)

Question 66

Rita is able to read 30 pages an hour. For an assignment she has two books to read. The first book has 1,350 pages and the second book has 2,010 pages. How many hours will it take Rita to finish both books?

a) 75   b) 110

c) 112   d) 121

Question 67

A car can accelerate at 5 kph per second. How much time will it take the car to reach 75 kph?

a) 15 seconds   b) 22 seconds

c) 25 seconds   d) 27 seconds

Question 68

John travels 75 KM to work each way. If he averages 120 kph, how many minutes does he spend driving to and from work each day?

a) 1.25   b) 75

c) 50   d) 60

Question 69

An officer's quota for speeding tickets each month is 0.5% of the average traffic flow on Highway 401. Each month the average flow is 13 million cars. If the officer has issued 50,000 tickets at mid-month, how many more tickets are needed to reach the quota?

a) 25,000   b) 15,000

c) 20,000   d) 30,000

Question 70

Students want to convert a spare room into a lab. The room space is 10' x 10'. A lab needs to have 120 square feet minimum for ventilation. How many more square feet are needed for this lab to be a "safe" environment to enter?

a) 30   b) 50

c) 40   d) 20

Question 71

A truck trailer is filled with explosives. The dimensions of the trailer are 25' x 10' x 15'. The explosives are in crates measuring 5' x 5' x 5'. How many crates of explosives can fit in the truck?

a) 27   b) 30

c) 42   d) 51

Question 72

There are 10 Caucasian, 14 African American and 12 Hispanic people in the office. If there are an equal number of men and women of each race, how many African American women are in the office?

a) 6   b) 7

c) 5   d) 18

Question 73

The average amount of snowfall in Maine increases by 6% each year. If the snowfall amount was 23 inches in 2001, what will the snowfall amount be in 2006?

a) 25.8 inches   b) 27.4 inches

c) 29.0 inches   d) 30.8 inches

Question 74

A park is planned and will be 3 city blocks by 3 city blocks in size. Each city block is 20 metres in length. What is the total area covered by the new park?

a) 1600 square metres   b) 2400 square metres

c) 3600 square metres   d) 4200 square metres

Question 75

A new, entry level employee makes $23,000 per year. If the salary level increases by 2% after every 3 years of service, what will her salary be after 8 years of work?

a) $23,460   b) $23,929

c) $24,408   d) $24,168

Question 76

Identify the synonym for the following words.

Irksome

a) Annoying   b) Irrational

c) Sour   d) Diseased

Question 77

Arraign

a) Sue   b) Confess

c) Exonerate   d) Prosecute

Question 78

Arduous

a) Clever   b) Emotional

c) Difficult   d) Thoughtful

Question 79
Perjury

a) Lying Under Oath   b) Testimony

c) Evidence   d) Selecting a Jury

Question 80
Pedestrians

a) Motorists   b) Toys

c) Athletes   d) Citizens on Foot

Question 81

What number should replace the asterisk in the following questions?

	32	18
154	23	9
145	14	*

a) 1   b) 3

c) 6   d) None of the above.

Question 82

21	63	*
3	9	27
	48	144

a) 81   b) 189

c) 154   d) None of the above.

Question 83

4	100	500
12	300	1500
	900	*

a) 3000   b) 3500

c) 4500   d) None of the above.

Question 84

3	12	48
	24	96
12	48	*

a) 192   b) 208

c) 480   d) None of the above.

Question 85

	3	18
2	6	*
4	12	72

a) 32

b) 36

c) 42

d) None of the above.

Question 86

What are the missing numbers in the following patterns?

1, ?, ?, 27, 81, 243, 729...

a) 3, 12

b) 4, 9

c) 3, 9

d) None of the above.

Question 87

2, ?, 4, 9, 6, 11, 8...

a) 6

b) 7

c) 8

d) None of the above.

Question 88

50, 0, 0, -40, -40, -70, -70, -90, -90, ?, ?...

a) -95, -100

b) -95, -95

c) -100, -100

d) None of the above.

Question 89

6, 16, 36, 76, 156, ?...

a) 316

b) 286

c) 356

d) None of the above.

Question 90

2, 4, ?, 256...

a) 12

b) 16

c) 20

d) None of the above.

1) A	26) A	51) A	76) A
2) D	27) B	52) B	77) D
3) C	28) B	53) B	78) C
4) B	29) C	54) D	79) A
5) C	30) B	55) D	80) D
6) A	31) C	56) C	81) D
7) B	32) A	57) B	82) B
8) D	33) B	58) C	83) C
9) A	34) A	59) D	84) A
10) C	35) B	60) A	85) B
11) C	36) A	61) B	86) C
12) E	37) B	62) C	87) B
13) A	38) C	63) C	88) C
14) E	39) C	64) B	89) A
15) B	40) B	65) G	90) B
16) H	41) D	66) C	
17) C	42) B	67) A	
18) E	43) C	68) B	
19) C	44) B	69) B	
20) H	45) D	70) D	
21) C	46) B	71) B	
22) C	47) C	72) B	
23) D	48) D	73) D	
24) D	49) D	74) C	
25) C	50) C	75) B	

Question 1

The children from the lowest to highest grade are: Michael, Robert, Jimmy, Lisa, Bonnie and then Rachael.

Question 2

The order of the horses from first to last is: solid brown, solid black, white with brown spots and then black with brown spots.

Question 3

The places of the girls on the beam from first to last are: Sarah, Amber and then Elaine.

Question 4

The order of employees, working from most to least, is: evening, morning, noon and then overnight.

Question 5

The women and their best-liked flower are as follows: Tina-Indian Paintbrush, Roberta-Rose, Veronica-daisy, Nancy-bluebonnets.

Question 6

The order that the girls could swim, from farthest to least, is: Christa, Nina, Tina, and then Gina.

Question 7

The order of water consumption from highest to lowest is: Ryan, Tom, Jim and then Bob.

Question 8

The girls with short hair are Veronica and Lisa, with medium hair are Britney and Julie, and with long hair are Courtney and Suzanne.

Question 9

Julie picks the orange tabby, Charlie picks the white Persian, Leslie picks the tan Siamese, and Danny picks the calico mix.

Question 10

The order of problems seen, from most to least, is: knee, neck, shoulder and then back.

Question 11

From left to right, the top left and bottom right line are lost. Then the top right and bottom left line are lost. Dots alternate from top to bottom to top on the top line, straight across on the middle line and bottom top bottom on the bottom line.

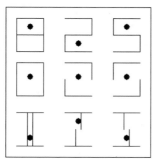

Question 12

An object from first row is superimposed on an object from the second row to create an object in the third row.

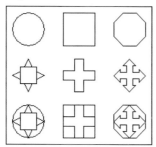

Question 13

Outside shapes remain consistent as you travel diagonally from top left to bottom right. Inside shapes remain consistent as you travel diagonally from top right to bottom left.

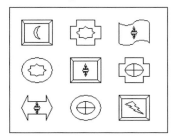

Question 14

The row consists of superimposing the middle row on the mirror image of the bottom row.

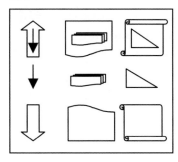

Question 15

Circles on outside represent positive integers; circles on the inside represent negative integers.

Row one is added to row two resulting in row three. $(3 - 1 = 2, 2 + 3 = 5, 5 - 4 = 1)$

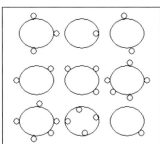

Question 16

The number of dots in the first row increase by one from left to right. The number of dots in the second row increase by two from left to right and by three in the third row.

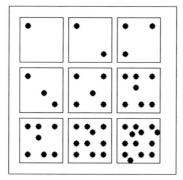

Question 17

To determine the third column, the shapes in the first column are added to the shapes in the second column. The black circles are covered by a black square in the third column, and the white circles are surrounded by another circle.

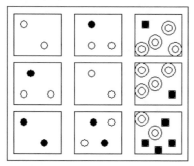

Question 18

The shapes from column one are superimposed on the shapes from column two which results in column three.

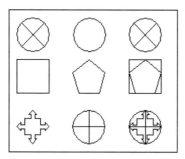

Question 19

A three-dimensional object in column one is followed by a two-dimensional object in column two, which is followed by a double image. Solid black shapes cross diagonally.

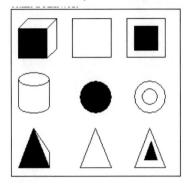

Question 20

The object in column one rotates 90 degrees clockwise in column two and a further 90 degrees in column three. The object that first appears in column two rotates 90 degrees clockwise in column three. The arrows that first appear in column three point in the opposite direction of the object that first appears in column two.

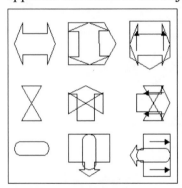

Question 21

To solve this problem, set up an algebraic equation. "Y" will represent the number of men and the number of women will equal y + 5. When you add the women to the men, the total is 75.

$y + y + 5 = 75$

$2y + 5 = 75$ Therefore, there are 35 men at the dance.

$2y = 70$

$y = 35$

Question 22

First, determine the total area of the canvas. 2m x 3m = 6 square metres.
Second, determine how much has been painted. 6 x 35% = 2.1 metres.
Finally, determine how much is left to be painted 6 – 2.1 = 3.9 square metres.

Question 23

Determine how much money is made in one week (38 x $6 = $228), and then multiply that total by the number of weeks ($228 x 3 = $684).

Question 24

600 x 15% = 90

Question 25

140 x 0.2 = 28 lbs. of cocaine. 140–28 = 112 lbs. remaining. 112/2 = 56 lbs. of marijuana.

Question 26

An algebraic equation will be required for this question.

$\dfrac{4\ km}{y\ km} = \dfrac{24\ minutes}{60\ minutes}$ Multiply both sides by "y". $4 = \dfrac{24\ y}{60}$

Multiply both sides by 60.   240 = 24 y   then divide both sides by 24.   10 = y

Stephen Chan was running at 10 km per hour.

Question 27

An algebraic equation will be required for this question.

$\dfrac{(7 - x)}{4} = x - 10$ Multiply both sides by 4. $7 - x = 4x - 40$

Add 40 to each side.   47 – x = 4x   Add y to both sides.   47 = 5x

Finally divide both sides by 5.   47/5 = x = 9.4.

Question 28

First, determine how many litres are drained each second. 44 litres / 60 seconds = 0.73. Therefore, 0.73 litres are drained from the sink each second.

Second, divide 0.73 litres into the 12 litre capacity of the sink. 0.73 / 12 = 16.4 seconds.

Question 29

First, calculate the total volume of the tank. 300 x 400 x 500 = 60,000,000 cubic cm. Second, determine the number of seconds that it will take to fill the tank. Divide the volume by the rate the water is flowing.
        6,000,000 / 20,000 = 3,000 minutes to fill the tank.
Finally, convert 3,000 seconds to minutes. 3,000 / 60 = 50 minutes to fill the tank.

Question 30

First, set up an algebraic equation where "y" represents the number of people who had a cola. ½ y would be the number of people who had lemonade.
        y + ½ y = 240 or 1.5 y = 240
To isolate "y" divide both sides by 1.5.
        y = 240/1.5 = 160 people were drinking cola.

Question 31

"Child" would be the most logical answer, as they would be most likely to chase the ball.

Question 32

"Gallant" is the correct answer, meaning courteous or chivalrous.

Question 33

A "catapult" is an older weapon that flung large rocks like missiles.

Question 34

"Neutral" means refusing to take sides.

Question 35

"Strain" is the most likely cause of a rope snapping.

Refer to the Answer Key for answers to questions 36-40

Question 41

Multiplying

	108	135	486
3	36	45	162
	12	15	27

Question 42

Adding → 2

	201	203	207
6	195	197	199
	189	191	193

Question 43

Multiplying → 4

	12	48	192
2	6	24	96
	3	12	48

Question 44

Multiplying → 3   6

	4	12	72
2	2	6	36
	1	3	18

Question 45

Adding 251

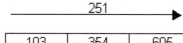

103	354	605
225	476	727
100	351	602

Question 46

The numbers are increasing by multiples of 2. (8, 16, 32, 64, 128, 256, 512...).

Question 47

The numbers are being added by 7. (-7. 0, 7, 14, 21, 28...).

Question 48

The numbers are declining by multiples of 3 in the following pattern: -3, -6, -9, -12 etc. (100, 97, 91, 82, 70, 55, ...)

Question 49

The numbers are being multiplied by 3 and then added by 2 (2, 8, 26, 80, 242...).

Question 50

The numbers are being multiplied by 2 and subtracted by 3 (9, 15, 27, 51, 99, 195...).

Question 51

If you spoke with the supplier four days ago and they advised the parts would be shipped in 6 days that means the parts will be shipped in 2 days. Add another 2 days for shipping and the answer is 4 days.

Question 52

The order of items, from most to least worn, is: short skirts, long skirts, shorts and then pants.

Question 53

The teams are in the following places, from first to last: Team 3, Team 2, Team 4, and then Team 1.

Question 54

The amount of paint needed by room, from most to least is: bedroom, dining room, kitchen, and then bathroom.

Question 55

Natalie handles fewer calls than Frank, so their combined total would not be as high as doubling Frank's production. Kristina, therefore, takes the most calls.

Question 56

If you go to school, ask questions, take the test and get A's, you will graduate next.

Question 57
The first letter of each word skips every second letter of the alphabet (A, C, E, G...)
Question 58
The first letter of each word skips a letter, then goes back one, then skips one, etc.

Question 59

Round brackets convert to curved brackets vertically. The same process is repeated horizontally.

Question 60

There are a declining number of rings on cord, while at the same time a doubling number of highlighted buttons.

Question 61

Expanding antenna, black circles traveling clockwise by one circle each image.

Question 62

Number of columns goes from 3,2,3,2. Number of black circles increasing by 1 each time (2,3,4,5).

Question 63

First two letters of the alphabet are followed by the last two. The next letters are the third and fourth letters of the alphabet followed by the third and fourth last letters of the alphabet. The next would be fifth and sixth letters of the alphabet, followed by the fifth and sixth last letters of the alphabet and so on…

Question 64

The middle column is a compressed merger of the first and second columns. The image from the first column is also rotated 180 degrees.

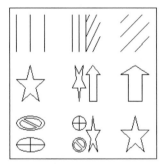

Question 65

The mages rotates 90 degrees between columns 1 and 2. Column 3 is a mirror image of column 2.

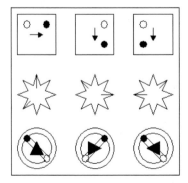

Question 66

First, calculate the total number of pages Rita must read [1,350 + 2,010 = 3,360]. Then, divide the total number pages by her reading speed [3,360/30 = 112 minutes].

Question 67

75/5=15   It will take 15 seconds to accelerate to 75 kph.

Question 68

Calculate John's total return trip driving distance [75 + 75 = 150KM]. Then divide total distance by his average driving speed [150/120=1.25hr]. Then convert 1.25 hours to minutes by multiplying by 60, to arrive at 75 minutes.

Question 69

13,000,000 x 0.005=65,000

65,000 - 50,000 = 15,000 tickets

Question 70

10 x 10 = 100 square feet

120 – 100 = 20 square feet

Question 71

25 x 10 x 15 = 3750 cubic feet

5 x 5 x 5 = 125 cubic feet

3750 / 125 = 30 boxes

Question 72

14 / 2 = 7

Question 73

2002: 23 x 1.06 = 24.38   2003: 24.38 x 1.06 = 25.84   2004: 25.84 x 1.06 = 27.39

2005: 27.39 x 1.06 = 29.036   2006: 29.036 x 1.06 = 30.8

Question 74

The perimeter would be 60 metres by 60 metres (20 x 3 = 60). The area would be 60 x 60 = 3600 square metres.

Question 75

Eight years of employment would provide 2 pay increases.

23,000 x 1.02 = $23,460   23,460 x 1.02 = $23,939

Refer to the Answer Key for answers to questions 76-80
Question 81

Adding

	163	32	18
9	154	23	9
	145	14	0

Question 82

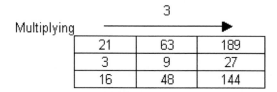

Multiplying

3		
21	63	189
3	9	27
16	48	144

Question 83

Multiplying

Question 84

Multiplying

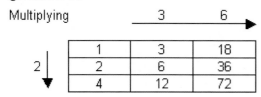

Question 85

Multiplying

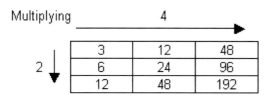

Question 86

The numbers are increasing by multiples of 3 (1, 3, 9, 27, 81, 243, 729...)

Question 87

The numbers grow by 5 then decrease by 3 (2, 7, 4, 9, 6, 11, 8...).

Question 88

The pattern is subtracting a declining multiple of 10 (50 then 40 then 30 etc.), followed by subtracting 0. -50, -0, -40, -0, -30, -0, -20, -0, etc. (50, 0, 0, -40, -40, -70, -70, -90, -90, -100, -100...).

Question 89

The numbers are being added by 2 and then multiplied by 2 (6, 16, 36, 76, 156, 316,...).

Question 90

The numbers are being squared (2, 4, 16, 256, 65536...).

148

WCPT

The Written Communication Proficiency Test (WCPT) measures an individual's ability to communicate in writing. These exams are used to assess employees (manager level) or leaders whose position requires them to write clear and concise letters, memos, reports or other documents. The test contains a number of short passages, which have errors and modified paragraphs that have to be corrected. There are a total of 50 multiple-choice questions in the following areas:

· Grammar
· Punctuation
· Fill in the blank
· Ordering sentences
· Reading comprehension

The test takes about 1 hour and 20 minutes to complete. If you are unsuccessful you must wait 180 days before you can rewrite the test.

Only paper, pencils and erasers are allowed - no books, dictionaries, notes, writing paper, calculators, calculator watches or other aids are permitted in the room.

Detach the answer key to take the test.

	A	B	C	D	
1)	○	○	○	○	___
2)	○	○	○	○	___
3)	○	○	○	○	___
4)	○	○	○	○	___
5)	○	○	○	○	___
6)	○	○	○	○	___
7)	○	○	○	○	___
8)	○	○	○	○	___
9)	○	○	○	○	___
10)	○	○	○	○	___

	A	B	C	D	
11)	○	○	○	○	___
12)	○	○	○	○	___
13)	○	○	○	○	___
14)	○	○	○	○	___
15)	○	○	○	○	___
16)	○	○	○	○	___
17)	○	○	○	○	___
18)	○	○	○	○	___
19)	○	○	○	○	___
20)	○	○	○	○	___

	A	B	C	D	
21)	○	○	○	○	___
22)	○	○	○	○	___
23)	○	○	○	○	___
24)	○	○	○	○	___
25)	○	○	○	○	___
26)	○	○	○	○	___
27)	○	○	○	○	___
28)	○	○	○	○	___
29)	○	○	○	○	___
30)	○	○	○	○	___

	A	B	C	D	
31)	○	○	○	○	___
32)	○	○	○	○	___
33)	○	○	○	○	___
34)	○	○	○	○	___
35)	○	○	○	○	___
36)	○	○	○	○	___
37)	○	○	○	○	___
38)	○	○	○	○	___
39)	○	○	○	○	___
40)	○	○	○	○	___

	A	B	C	D	
41)	○	○	○	○	___
42)	○	○	○	○	___
43)	○	○	○	○	___
44)	○	○	○	○	___
45)	○	○	○	○	___
46)	○	○	○	○	___
47)	○	○	○	○	___
48)	○	○	○	○	___
49)	○	○	○	○	___
50)	○	○	○	○	___

Read the following paragraphs and answer the questions.

Paragraph A

(1)The main concern these citizen's have is the removal of barriers, but this legislation wouldn't provide these citizen's with the remedy _____ long been waiting for. (2)The bill would require municipalities, schools, transit systems, hospitals, universities and colleges to develop plans that identify barriers in their policies and programs. (3)There's no requirement for these bodies to implement their plans or set deadlines to eliminate the barriers.

Paragraph B

(4)Jill Givens pledged more than two-years ago to enact legislation knocking down the barriers that stand in the way of people with disabilities. (5)The bill will be introduced next year. (6)It is a step in the right direction, but it will need _____ amendment to bring about the changes demanded by the 1.6 million Canadians with disabilities. (7)The proposed law would raise public awareness of the many barriers that impede people with disabilities from working, going to school or simply _____ a normal life.

Paragraph C

(8)Nor does the new Disabilities Act go beyond encouraging the private sector to make facilities, and services more accessible. (9)Nothing will happen if moral persuasion fails. (10)Provincial officials and community advocates agree that part of the problem is the lack of common standards to define accessibility. (11)Two new councils will be created to set such standards and advise the government on future initiatives.

Question 1

Which of the following alternatives is the right order of the three paragraphs of the text?

a) A, C, B

b) B, A, C

c) B, C, A

d) C, A, B

Question 2

Which of the following is the most appropriate title for the text?

a) A Final Solution to Disability Issues

b) Total Barrier Elimination

c) Awareness But Not Enough Action

d) Canada's Political Agenda

Question 3

Which of the following rephrases of Sentence 4 is best in terms of style and conciseness?

a) The legislation being knocked down was pledged by Jill Givens two years ago for people with disabilities.

b) People with disabilities pledged more than two years ago to enact legislation knocking down the barriers that stand in their way.

c) Knocking down barriers that stand in the way of people with disabilities by changing legislation has been a promise of Jill Givens for more than two years.

d) Jill Givens enacted legislation more than two years ago knocking down the barriers that stand in the way of people with disabilities.

Question 4

Which of the following words, if inserted in the blank in Sentence 6, would best fit the style of the sentence in the whole text?

a) Substantial   b) Big

c) Infinitesimal   d) Gargantuan

Question 5

Which of the following phrases, if added in the blank in Sentence 7, would best fit the meaning of the paragraph?

a) sharing   b) being

c) leading   d) belonging

Question 6

Which of the following changes is needed in the text?

a) Sentence 6: change the comma after direction to a semicolon.

b) Sentence 1: change citizen's to citizens.

c) Sentence 7: change raise to rise.

d) Sentence 11: replace Two with Too

Question 7

Which of the following changes would improve the text?

a) Sentence 2: add a comma after policies.

b) Sentence 3: remove the apostrophe in the word there's.

c) Sentence 4: add dashes to the words people-with-disabilities.

d) Sentence 8: remove the comma after the word facilities.

Question 8

Where would you most likely find this article?

a) Training Manual   b) Newspaper

c) Design Magazine   d) Sales Brochure

Question 9

Which of the following changes would improve the text?

a) Sentence 4: remove the dash between two-years.

b) Sentence 7: remove the comma after working.

c) Sentence 8: add an apostrophe to the word disabilities.

d) Sentence 11: add an apostrophe to the word councils

Question 10

What is the best word to replace the blank space in sentence 1?

a) that has

b) have

c) they've

d) they're

Read the following three paragraphs and answer the ensuing questions based on what you have read.

Paragraph A

(1) Beset by a troubled administration and serious financial woes that could mean tax hikes or service cuts, Edmonton needs a top _____ who can provide a steady hand on the tiller. (2) A city search committee has unanimously picked Jeff Harris to be the new chief administrative officer. (3) Counsel should enthusiastically endorse this choice; when it debates the issue in counsel this week.

Paragraph B

(4) Harris's former work in the City of Calgary, his term as commissioner of community and neighbourhood services with Edmonton and his most recent job as interim chief administrative officer give him strong qualifications to take on this big job. (5) "He has the mettle and the smarts to manage a city with a $4 billion operating budget and 18,000 employees."

Paragraph C

(6) He has the backbone to make hard decisions and the sensitivity to ensure that the vulnerable _____ not victimized. (7) Harris has earned the respect of staff and counsellors alike and has a good rapport with Mayor Bing, something that his _____, Janet Dawson, never enjoyed, which ultimately led to her departure in March. (8) Unlike someone hired from outside the province, Harris is already well acquainted with the personalities and issues at City Hall. (9) If selected, Harris would take on the job with a "to do" list already filled with tasks.

Question 11

Which of the following words, if inserted in the blank in Sentence 7, would best fit the style of the sentence in the whole text?

a) enemy

b) pal

c) predecessor

d) alias

Question 12

Which of the following words, if inserted in the blank in Sentence 1, would best fit the style of the sentence in the whole text?

a) debater

b) bureaucrat

c) man

d) parliamentarian

Question 13

Which of the following words, if inserted in the blank in Sentence 6, would best fit the style of the sentence in the whole text?

a) are

b) is

c) were

d) can

Question 14

Which of the following alternatives is the right order of the three paragraphs of the text?

a) A, B, C   b) C, A, B

c) B, C, A   d) B, A, C

Question 15

Which of the following would be the best title for the article?

a) Fixing Corruption   b) Searching for Leadership

c) Edmonton Politics   d) A Welcome Change to the Helm

Question 16

Where would this article most likely be displayed in a newspaper?

a) Political Editorial Section   b) Provincial Affairs Section

c) Municipal Affairs Section   d) National Affairs Section

Question 17

Which of the following rephrases of Sentence 2 is best in terms of style and conciseness?

a) Jeff Harris picked himself unanimously as the new chief administrative officer by a city search committee.

b) The new chief administrative officer would best be filled by Jeff Harris.

c) Jeff Harris was unanimously picked by a city search committee as the new chief administrative officer.

d) A city search committee unanimously picked their new chief administrative officer. The new chief administrative officer is going to be Jeff Harris.

Question 18

Which of the following changes is needed in the text?

a) Sentence 4: The word chief should be spelled cheif.

b) Sentence 3: The word counsel should be spelled council.

c) Sentence 5: The words operating budget should be replaced with financing budget.

d) Sentence 7: The word rapport should be replaced with the word report.

Question 19

Which of the following changes would improve the text?

a) Sentence 3: There should be no semi-colon after the word choice.

b) Sentence 4: There should be no apostrophe in the word Harris's.

c) Sentence 4: There should be no comma after the word Calgary.

d) Sentence 5: There should be a comma after the word mettle.

Question 20

Which of the following changes would improve the text?

a) Sentence 7: There should be no comma after Mayor Bing.

b) Sentence 5: There should not be quotation marks around the sentence.

c) Sentence 7: The word March should not be capitalized.

d) Sentence 9: There should be a comma added after the word list.

Read the following paragraphs and answer the questions.

Paragraph A

(1)The commission did however vote to close an Air Force base in Brunswick Maine. (2)Citizens in the area wanted to simply reduce the number of personnel at this location. (3)It was _____ by the commission that the base needed to be closed.

Paragraph B

(4)Many over the past few months have been worried that the plans to scale down the military would leave the New England states _____. (5)Many feel that if the New England areas are _____ down they will not be able to be brought back.

Paragraph C

(6)Two New England locations were kept open during the Pentagon's talks about scaling back military bases. (7)The locations were the shipyard in Kittery, Maine and a submarine base in connecticut. (8)These are considerd the economic backbone of the region by many living there.

Question 21

What would be the most logical order of the paragraphs in this selection?

a) A,B,C   b) B,C,A

c) C,A,B   d) A,C,B

Question 22

Which would be considered the most appropriate title for this selection?

a) New England Punished   b) Pentagon Talks

c) Military Base Closures   d) Storms Hit Hard

Question 23

Where would this selection most likely be found?

a) Newspaper   b) Scientific Journal

c) Textbook   d) Short Story

Question 24

Which of the following rephrases of Sentence 8 is best in terms of style and conciseness?

a) The places are going to be the best ones to keep open.

b) The regions are important economic areas for the country.

c) The places should be left open since people like to visit them so much and tourist dollars are created.

d) The locations are thought by many to be the economic foundation for the region.

Question 25

Which of the following changes would improve the text?

a) Sentence 2: there should be a comma after the word area.

b) Sentence 1: add a comma between Brunswick and Maine.

c) Sentence 6: there should not be an apostrophe on the word Pentagon's.

d) Sentence 8: add an exclamation mark after the word there.

Question 26

Which of the following words, if inserted into the blank in Sentence 3, would best fit the style of the sentence in the whole text?

a) Allowed.

b) Listen.

c) Left.

d) Voted.

Question 27

Which of the following changes would improve the text?

a) Sentence 2: personnel should be replaced with personal.

b) Sentence 2: change the "c" to a lower case in Citizens.

c) Sentence 7: change the "c" to a capital in connecticut.

d) Sentence 8: change the word there to their.

Question 28

Which of the following words, if inserted into the blank in Sentence 4, would best fit the style of the sentence in the whole text?

a) Charged.

b) Vulnerable.

c) Eradicated.

d) Decimated.

Question 29

Which of the following changes would improve the text?

a) Sentence 8: Considerd should be spelled considered.

b) Sentence 1: Commission should be spelled comission.

c) New England should be spelled New – England throughout.

d) Sentence 7: Maine should be spelled Mane.

Question 30

Which of the following words, if inserted into the blank in Sentence 5, would best fit the style of the sentence in the whole text?

a) Replaced.

b) Scaled.

c) Habituated.

d) Relieved.

Read the following three paragraphs and answer the ensuing questions based on what you have read.

Paragraph A

(1)There is a new hurricane brewing in the atlantic ocean. (2)There are sustained winds at: 39 miles per hour and it is moving at 7 miles per hour. (3)Florida is the first location that will be hit.

Paragraph B

(4)The next place the hurricane should make landfall is Louisiana. (5)By this point, it should be a Category 2 storm. (6)People in Louisiana and Texas are _____ to begin taking precautions now.

Paragraph C

(7)Once landfall is made in Louisiana; the storm is expected to wear itself down and not make it much farther north than the middle of Louisiana. (8)Areas north of this location are being _____ to allow evacuees to take up _____ in their towns.

Question 31

Which of the following changes would improve the text?

a) Sentence 8: capitalize the word north.

b) Sentence 7: Wear should be spelled where.

c) Sentence 7: landfall should be two words - land fall.

d) Sentence 1: capitalize the words atlantic and ocean.

Question 32

Which would be considered the most appropriate title for this selection?

a) Death and Fury are Headed This Way.

b) Batten Down the Hatches Georgia.

c) Latest Hurricane in the Atlantic.

d) Ravages of Mother Nature.

Question 33

Which of the following rephrases of Sentence 6 is best in terms of style and conciseness?

a) Citizens preparing for the hurricane of Louisiana and Texas are cautioned that now is the best time to begin hurricane precautions.

b) Citizens of Louisiana and Texas are cautioned that now is the best time to begin hurricane precautions.

c) Citizens of Louisiana and Texas are to begin preparing.

d) Citizens of Louisiana and Texas are cautioned by the mayor and the president, that now is the best time to begin hurricane precautions.

Question 34

Which of the following changes would improve the text?

a) Sentence 2: remove the colon after the word at.

b) Sentence 3: capitalize the "f" in first.

c) Sentence 4: an exclamation mark should be used after Louisiana.

d) Sentence 7: change than to then.

Question 35

In which section of the newspaper would this selection be found?

a) Classified section.   b) Sports section.

c) Business section.   d) Weather section.

Question 36

Which of the following words, if inserted into the blank in Sentence 6, would best fit the style of the sentence in the whole text?

a) Persuaded.   b) Encouraged.

c) Demanded.   d) Discouraged.

Question 37

Which of the following changes would improve the text?

a) Sentence 4: add a comma after the word landfall.

b) Sentence 5: remove the comma after the word point.

c) Sentence 7: replace the semicolon with a comma after the word Louisiana.

d) Sentence 8: add quotation marks around this sentence.

Question 38

What would be the most logical order of the paragraphs in this selection?

a) C,B,A   b) A,B,C

c) A,C,B   d) C,A,B

Question 39

Which of the following words, if inserted into the blanks in Sentence 8, would best fit the style of the sentence in the whole text?

a) Mandated and place.   b) Order and citizenship.

c) Urged and residence.   d) Required and citizenship.

Question 40

Where would this selection most likely be found?

a) Scientific Journal.   b) Short Story.

c) Sales Pamphlet.   d) Newspaper.

Read the following paragraphs and answer the ensuing questions based on what you have read.

Paragraph A

(1) Medicine, communication and leisure are just three areas of our lives that have improved because of computers. (2) The advantages they have brought, in my opinion, far outweigh any disadvantages.

Paragraph B

(3) Computer technology has _____ increased the opportunities that sick and disabled people have to lead normal lives. (4) For example, blind people can now use a laser beam to help them work out how far they are from objects. (5) Computers have also helped people who live in isolated areas to get medical help quickly in an emergency. (6) X-rays and brain scans of patients a long way away can be looked at by specialists in big city hospitals by use of computers linked to modems. (7) They can then give instructions to hospital staff about what to do. (8) Sometimes this can save lives.

Paragraph C

(9) In communication, one of the things that has changed our lives immensely has been the Internet. (10) Businesses these days cannot survive without being connected to the Internet. (11) If someone in an office on the other side of the world needs to send a document to someone in Britain, it would take days without a computer. (12) But thanks to the Internet it can be done in a matter of seconds by email. (13) Email has changed our personal lives too. (14) Even grandparents around the world are "logging-on" to talk to their young grandchildren far away.

Paragraph D

(15) It is difficult for most people to imagine life without computers. (16) Even if we do not have a computer in our homes, computers are now a major part of our lives. (17) Among the many areas where they have brought benefits are medicine, communication and leisure.

Paragraph E

(18) Leisure is another aspect of everyday life that computers have improved. (19) Many children get great enjoyment out of the many interesting and challenging computer games they can play. (20) Although there are many games that involve violence, if the games are chose carefully they can really help children develop thinking skills and quick reflexes. (21) Also when we sit down to watch a sports game on television, it is computers that bring us the many different camera angles, instant action replays and tallies of penalties.

Question 41

Which of the following questions would this essay most likely be addressing?

a) What are some of the advantages and disadvantages of computers?

b) Discuss how computers are taking over our lives.

c) What are the benefits of computers?

d) Discuss some major changes taking place in the medical, communication and leisure industries.

Question 42

Which of the following is an example used in the essay on how disabled people are aided by a computer?

a) Blind people can use laser beams to help guide them.

b) Specialists can view X-rays from long distances using modems.

c) Video games can help improve reflexes.

d) All of the above.

Question 43

This sentence is missing from the text. Where does it belong?
People in wheelchairs can easily drive and control their chairs without help from anyone else.

a) Before the first sentence in Paragraph B.

b) Before the second sentence in Paragraph B.

c) Before the third sentence in Paragraph B.

d) Before the fourth sentence in Paragraph B.

Question 44

Which of the following is a negative aspect of computers mentioned in the essay?

a) Difficulty sending files around the world.

b) Violent video games.

c) Poor communication between generations.

d) Lack of professional people in rural areas.

Question 45

What two areas of life does the essay focus on when discussing changes in communication?

a) Business and email.

b) Business and grandparents.

c) Grandparents and email.

d) Business and personal life.

Question 46

Which sentence of the introduction tells the reader exactly what the paragraphs will be about?

a) First

b) Second

c) Third

d) Fourth

Question 47

Which of the following alternatives is the right order of the five paragraphs of the text?

a) D, E, C, B, A

b) A, C, B, D, E

c) A, B, C, E, D

d) D, B, C, E, A

Question 48

Which of the following rephrases of Sentence 6 is best in terms of style and conciseness?

a) Specialists in big city hospitals can use computers linked to modems to look at X-rays and brain scans of patients a long way away.

b) X-rays and brain scans of patients a long way away can be looked at by specialists in big city hospitals by use of computers linked to modems.

c) In big city hospitals, specialists can use computers to look at X-rays and brain scans of patients a long way away linked to modems.

d) X-rays and brain scans of patients can be looked at by specialists in big city hospitals a long way away by use of computers linked to modems.

Question 49

Which of the following changes need to be made to the essay?

a) Sentence 3 – change opportunities to opportunitie's.

b) Sentence 14 – change grandchildren to grand children.

c) Sentence 17 – add a comma after the word communication.

d) Sentence 20 – change are chose to are chosen.

Question 50

What is the best word to replace the blank space in sentence 3?

a) marginally

b) dramatically

c) progressive

d) substantial

1) B	26) D
2) C	27) C
3) C	28) B
4) A	29) A
5) C	30) B
6) B	31) D
7) D	32) C
8) B	33) B
9) A	34) A
10) C	35) D
11) C	36) B
12) B	37) C
13) A	38) B
14) A	39) C
15) D	40) D
16) A	41) C
17) C	42) A
18) B	43) C
19) A	44) B
20) B	45) D
21) B	46) C
22) C	47) D
23) A	48) A
24) D	49) D
25) B	50) B

Question 1

The first sentence of paragraph A refers back to the citizens in paragraph B. The opening line in paragraph C continues from the last sentence in paragraph A.

Question 2

"A Final Solution to Disability Issues" and " Total Barrier Elimination" would be inappropriate as the article suggests that people with disabilities are not happy with these initial steps. "Canada's Political Agenda" is too vague of a title.

Question 3

The first sentence is incorrect because legislation is not being knocked down. The second sentence is incorrect because Jill Givens made the pledge. The forth sentence is incorrect because the legislation was not enacted two years ago. Option three is correct because it contains all the pertinent information without being redundant.

Question 4

"Big" is too informal for the article. "Infinitesimal" has an incorrect meaning because the implication is that the changes required are large in nature. "Gargantuan" does not fit the style of the article.

Question 5

"Leading" is the correct answer as it completes the expression appropriately.

Question 6

The word "citizens" in sentence 1 is not expressing ownership and does not require an apostrophe.

Question 7

There is no need for a comma after the word "facilities".

Question 8

The style of the article best resembles that found in a newspaper.

Question 9

There is no need to hyphenate the words two years, as they are separate words.

Question 10

"That has" is incorrect as it would not agree with the verb "waiting". "Have" would not make grammatical or logical sense. "They're" does not agree with the tense of the sentence. "They've" is the best answer.

Question 11

"Enemy" is inappropriate as it is too harsh and probably untrue. "Pal" is too informal for this article. "Alias" would not make sense. "Predecessor" is the best answer.

Question 12

"Debater" is not the position that is being filled. "Man" would be inappropriate and sexist in this article. "Parliamentarian" would be too formal and an incorrect position. "Bureaucrat" is the best answer.

Question 13

"Are" is the grammatically correct word because it agrees with the present tense of the sentence and the plural subject "the vulnerable".

Question 14

A, B, C is the best solution. Jeff Harris is introduced in paragraph A, so it should be the first paragraph.

Question 15

"A Welcome Change to the Helm" is the best answer because it reflects the feeling of the article that the newly-appointed position is well filled.

Question 16

This article is full of opinion, which is typically found in the editorial section.

Question 17

Sentence 1 is incorrect, as Jeff did not pick himself. Sentence 2 is vague about how he was picked. Sentence 4 contains redundant information. Sentence 3 is the best selection.

Question 18

The word "counsel" means advice. The proper word for sentence 3 is "council", meaning political committee.

Question 19

There is no need for a semi-colon after the word "choice". A semi-colon is used to combine two independent clauses. Sentence three has an independent and a dependent clause.

Question 20

Quotation marks around sentence 5 are inappropriate, as the sentence is not a quotation from a speaker in the article.

Question 21

B,C,A is the best solution. The main idea is introduced in Paragraph B. The two locations that were kept open are mentioned in Paragraph C and the closing Paragraph is A.

Question 22

Military Base Closures is the best answer as it sums up the main idea of the article.

Question 23

This article is a current event notice, so it would be found in a newspaper.

Question 24

Option 1 is incorrect because it does not give any of the original information. Option 2 is incorrect as it does not follow the general style of the piece and has inaccurate information. Option 3 is incorrect as it has inaccurate information. Option 4 is correct because it restates the original information accurately.

Question 25

There should be a comma between the city and state.

Question 26

"Voted" is the only action word listed that would complete the sentence to portray the activity that occurred.

Question 27

Option 1 is not correct because New England should be capitalized. Option 2 is not correct because the first letter of a sentence should be capitalized. Option 4 is not correct because Pentagon is a proper name and should be capitalized. Option 3 is correct because Connecticut is a proper name and should be capitalized.

Question 28

"Vulnerable" means susceptible to emotional harm so it describes how the action will affect the people of the area.

Question 29

The past tense of "consider" requires the ending "-ed".

Question 30

"Scaled" is the appropriate word as the expression "scaled down" means reduced.

Question 31

Option 1 is incorrect because "north" is being used as a direction rather than a location. Option 2 is incorrect because "where" indicates a destination. Option 3 is incorrect because "landfall" is one word. Option 4 is correct because Atlantic Ocean is a proper noun and should be capitalized.

Question 32

Options 1 and 4 are too extreme as the hurricane will not be a strong one. Option 2 is not correct because the hurricane is not predicted to hit Georgia. Option 3 is correct because it gives a quick statement about the article's content.

Question 33

Option 1 contains redundant information. Option 3 is vague and doesn't contain enough information. Option 4 contains information that is not included in the original sentence. Option 2 is the correct answer.

Question 34

Option 2 is incorrect because "first" doesn't need to be capitalized. Option 3 is incorrect because no exclamation mark is required. Option 4 is incorrect because "than" is required in a comparison. Option 1 is correct because the colon needs to be used to start a list and there is no list here.

Question 35

Option 4 is correct because it is where the latest weather-related information is found.

Question 36

Option 2 is correct because the article is encouraging people to begin to take some action. The words "persuaded", "demanded" and "discouraged" would not fit the tone of the article.

Question 37

Option 1 is incorrect because there is no need for a comma. Option 2 is incorrect as the comma belongs after the word "point". Option 4 is incorrect as the sentence is not a statement being made by a particular person. Option 3 is correct as the appropriate punctuation mark here is a comma rather than a semicolon.

Question 38

A,B,C is the most logical order because Paragraph A begins by telling where the storm currently is. Paragraph B explains where the hurricane will go next. Paragraph C explains what will happen when it is over land.

Question 39

Option 1 is incorrect because "place" would not fit in with the sentence. Options 2 and 4 are incorrect because evacuees would probably already be citizens. Option 3 is the correct answer because the past tense "urged" and "residence" complete the sentence logically.

Question 40

The selection would be in the newspaper because it is a recent event. The other options are less likely to carry a story that changes so often.

Question 41

Even though the essay focuses on the medical, communication and leisure industries, the main topic of the essay is the benefits of computers.

Question 42

The only disabled people discussed in the text, who use computers with laser beams to determine how far they are away from different objects.

Question 43

The first sentence of the paragraph would be the introductory sentence. The second sentence beginning with "For example" is a good transition from the first and second sentence. The third sentence marks a transition from disabled people to a new issue of rural medicine, so this sentence should be added before the third sentence.

Question 44

The essay states that computers make sending files around the world and communication easier, not more difficult and the article does not discuss computers having an impact on lack of people in rural areas.

Question 45

The two main areas the essay focuses on are business and communication. Grandparents, and email are examples of the personal life.

Question 46

The third sentence states: "…brought benefits are medicine, communication and leisure."

Question 47

The essay should be written with the introduction, followed by paragraphs on medicine, communication, leisure and finally a conclusion according to the introductory paragraph.

Question 48

Answers A and D are both in passive voice and are not as well written as option B. Option C is inappropriate as it confusingly implies that patients, and not computers are linked by modem.

Question 49

The appropriate verb form in sentence 20 is "if the games are chose carefully".

Question 50

An adverb is required describing the verb increased. The essay is discussing the significant gains that computers have created in life, so the word dramatically would be a better fit with the mood of the essay.

eCFAT

The electronic Canadian Forces Aptitude Test (eCFAT) is used to help determine specific Military Occupations for which you are best suited. There are three components to the test.
- · Verbal Skills - 15 questions / 5 minutes
- · Spatial Ability - 15 questions / 10 minutes
- · Problem Solving - 30 questions / 30 minutes

Only paper, pencils and erasers are allowed - no books, dictionaries, notes, writing paper, calculators, calculator watches or other aids are permitted in the room.

Detach the answer sheet to take the test.

Answer Sheet eCFAT

Verbal Test

	A	B	C	D				A	B	C	D	E	F	
1)	○	○	○	○	___		9)	○	○	○	○	○	___
2)	○	○	○	○	___		10)	○	○	○	○	○	___
3)	○	○	○	○	___		11)	○	○	○	○	○	___
4)	○	○	○	○	___		12)	○	○	○	○	○	___
5)	○	○	○	○	___		13)	○	○	○	○	○	___
6)	○	○	○	○	___		14)	○	○	○	○	○	___
7)	○	○	○	○	___		15)	○	○	○	○	○	___
8)	○	○	○	○	___								

Total ____ / 15

Spatial Test

	A	B	C	D			A	B	C	D			A	B	C	D	
1)	○	○	○	○		13)	○	○	○	○	___	25)	○	○	○	○	___
2)	○	○	○	○	___	14)	○	○	○	○	___	26)	○	○	○	○	___
3)	○	○	○	○	___	15)	○	○	○	○	___	27)	○	○	○	○	___
4)	○	○	○	○	___	16)	○	○	○	○	___	28)	○	○	○	○	___
5)	○	○	○	○	___	17)	○	○	○	○	___	29)	○	○	○	○	___
6)	○	○	○	○	___	18)	○	○	○	○	___	30)	○	○	○	○	___
7)	○	○	○	○	___	19)	○	○	○	○	___	31)	○	○	○	○	___
8)	○	○	○	○	___	20)	○	○	○	○	___	32)	○	○	○	○	___
9)	○	○	○	○	___	21)	○	○	○	○	___	33)	○	○	○	○	___
10)	○	○	○	○	___	22)	○	○	○	○	___	34)	○	○	○	○	___
11)	○	○	○	○	___	23)	○	○	○	○	___	35)	○	○	○	○	___
12)	○	○	○	○	___	24)	○	○	○	○	___					

Total ____ / 35

Problem Solving Test

	A	B	C	D	E	F			A	B	C	D			A	B	C	D	
1)	○	○	○	○			___	11)	○	○	○	○	___	21)	○	○	○	○	___
2)	○	○	○	○			___	12)	○	○	○	○	___	22)	○	○	○	○	___
3)	○	○	○	○			___	13)	○	○	○	○	___	23)	○	○	○	○	___
4)	○	○	○	○	E	F		14)	○	○	○	○	___	24)	○	○	○	○	___
5)	○	○	○	○	○	○	___	15)	○	○	○	○	___	25)	○	○	○	○	___
6)	○	○	○	○	○	○	___	16)	○	○	○	○	___	26)	○	○	○	○	___
7)	○	○	○	○	○	○	___	17)	○	○	○	○	___	27)	○	○	○	○	___
8)	○	○	○	○	○	○	___	18)	○	○	○	○	___	28)	○	○	○	○	___
9)	○	○	○	○	○	○	___	19)	○	○	○	○	___	29)	○	○	○	○	___
10)	○	○	○	○			___	20)	○	○	○	○	___	30)	○	○	○	○	___

Total ____ / 30   **Total ____ / 80**

Question 1

Expendable means:

a) Able to Grow   b) Disposable

c) Careful   d) Watchful

Question 2

Abominable means:

a) Hateful   b) Snowman

c) Violent   d) A bomb

Question 3

Mystique means:

a) Foggy   b) Air of Mystery

c) Failed   d) Began

Question 4

Commenced means:

a) Finished   b) Graduation

c) Failed   d) Began

Question 5

Daunting means:

a) Extensive   b) Developed

c) Charming   d) Discouraging

Question 6

Pigment means:

a) Colouring Agent   b) Young Pig

c) Stupid   d) Stubborn

Question 7

Forlorn means:

a) Worn Out   b) Joyful

c) Dejected   d) Grassy Quadrangle

Question 8

Vicious means:

a) Sticky   b) Ferocious

c) Short   d) Fast

Question 9

Which two words have the opposite meaning?

a) Credible　　b) Untrustworthy　　c) Challenging　　d) Careful

a) a & b　　b) a & c　　c) a & d

d) b & c　　e) b & d　　f) c & d

Question 10

Which two words have the opposite meaning?

a) Opposite　　b) Premature　　c) Alike　　d) Gentle

a) a & b　　b) a & c　　c) a & d

d) b & c　　e) b & d　　f) c & d

Question 11

Which two words have the opposite meaning?

a) Grant　　b) Praise　　c) Condemn　　d) Harden

a) a & b　　b) a & c　　c) a & d

d) b & c　　e) b & d　　f) c & d

Question 12

Which two words have the opposite meaning?

a) Replenish　　b) Reuse　　c) Empty　　d) Taint

a) a & b　　b) a & c　　c) a & d

d) b & c　　e) b & d　　f) c & d

Question 13

Which two words have the same meaning?

a) Strong　　b) Harmful　　c) Frail　　d) Delicate

a) a & b　　b) a & c　　c) a & d

d) b & c　　e) b & d　　f) c & d

Question 14

Which two words have the same meaning?

a) Toil　　b) Enigma　　c) Grow　　d) Labour

a) a & b　　b) a & c　　c) a & d

d) b & c　　e) b & d　　f) c & d

Question 15

Which two words have the opposite meaning?

a) Tall　　b) Wide　　c) Large　　d) Narrow

a) a & b　　b) a & c　　c) a & d

d) b & c　　e) b & d　　f) c & d

Question 1

A   B   C   D

Question 2

A   B   C   D

Question 3

A   B   C   D

Question 4

A   B   C   D

Question 5

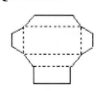

A   B   C   D

Question 6

A   B   C   D

Question 7

A   B   C   D

Question 8

A   B   C   D

Question 9

A   R   C   D

Question 10

A   B   C   D

Question 11

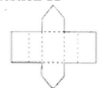

A   B   C   D

Question 12

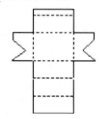

A   B   C   D

Question 13

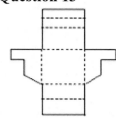

A   B   C   D

Question 14

A   B   C   D

Question 15

A   B   C   D

Question 16

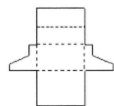

A   B   C   D

Question 17

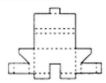

A   B   C   D

Question 18

A   B   C   D

Question 19

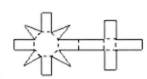

A   B   C   D

Question 20

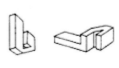

A   B   C   D

Question 21

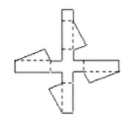

A   B   C   D

Question 22

 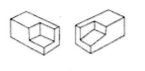

A   B   C   D

Question 23

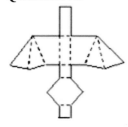

A   B   C   D

Question 24

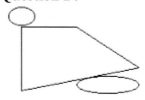

A   B   C   D

Question 25

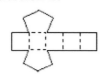

A   B   C   D

Question 26

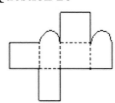

A   B   C   D

Question 27

 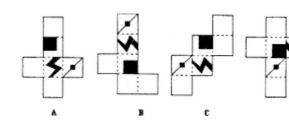

A   B   C   D

Question 28

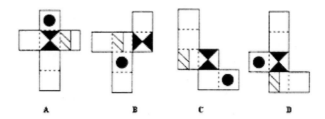

A   **B**   **C**   **D**

Question 29

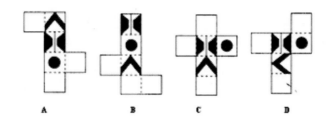

A   **B**   **C**   **D**

Question 30

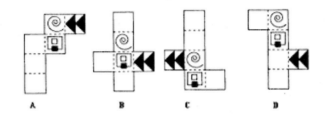

A   **B**   **C**   **D**

Question 31

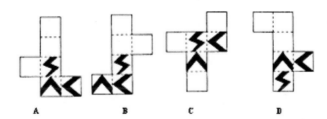

A   **B**   **C**   **D**

Question 32

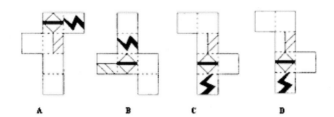

A   **B**   **C**   **D**

Question 33

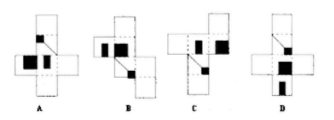

A   **B**   **C**   **D**

Question 34

A   B   C   D

Question 35

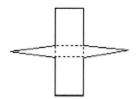

A   B   C   D

Question 1

521 x 346 =

a) 123 566   b) 150 326   c) 180 266   d) none of these

Question 2

What time is it in Toronto when it is 1 pm Eastern Standard time in Melbourne? Melbourne time is 16 hours ahead of Toronto's time.

a) 9 pm   b) 9 am   c) 7 am   d) 7 pm

Question 3

How much change would James receive after paying $50.00 for the following products:

    6 packets of crackers at $3.54 a packet
    5 kg of oranges at $1.95 a kilogram
    3 dozen muffins at $3.75 per dozen

a) $42.24   b) $24.16   c) $7.76   d) none of these

Question 4

Which of the following represents fractions arranged in a decreasing order of size?

a) 0.003, 0.02, 0.1   b) 2/3, 1/4, 13/15, 3/5, 5/1

c) 15/16, 7/8, 3/4, 2/3, ½   d) none of the above

Which is the missing image in the patterns below?
Question 5

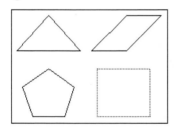

a)

b)

c)

d)

e)

f)

Question 6

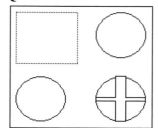

a)

b)

c)

d)

e)

f)

Question 7

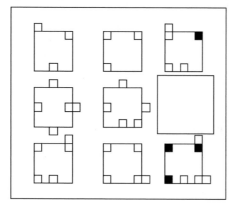

a)

b)

c)

d)

e)

f)

Question 8

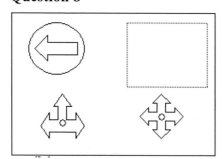

a)

b)

c)

d)

e)

f)

Question 9

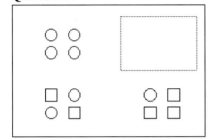

a) ○ △
   △ □

b) ○ □
   □ □

c) ○ ○
   □ ○

d) ○ □
   ○ □

e) ○ □
   △ □

f) ○ □
   □ ○

What are the missing numbers in the following patterns?

Question 10

33, ?, 29, 27, 25, ?...

a) 31, 23   b) 32, 24   c) 30, 24   d) None of these.

Question 11

-4, ?, -16, 32, -64, 128, ?...

a) -8, -256   b) 8, -256   c) 8, 256   d) None of these.

Question 12

2, 9, 23, ?, 107, ...

a) 47   b) 51   c) 53   d) None of these.

Question 13

89, ?, 87, 86, ?, 84, 83...

a) 88 and 81   b) 88 and 83   c) 87 and 85   d) None of these.

Question 14

7, 11, 19, 35, 67, ?, 259...

a) 134   b) 117   c) 131   d) None of these.

Question 15

A man punches into work at 1:45 pm and punches out at 3:30 am. How long was his shift?

a) 1:45   b) 10:30   c) 13:30   d) None of these.

Question 16

6 ½ minus 3 ¾ plus 4 ½ equals

a) 7 ½   b) 7 ¼   c) 7 ¾   d) None of these.

Question 17

A crate full of wheat weighs 60 kg. If 4 1/3 kg of wheat is spilled out of the crate, how much does the remaining wheat weigh?

a) 55 1/3   b) 55 2/3   c) 56 2/3   d) None of these.

Question 18

What number if doubled, gives you one quarter of 32?

a) 4   b) 8   c) 12   d) None of these.

Replace the asterisk with the missing number in the following questions.

Question 19

1	2	8
3	6	*
9		72

a) 16   b) 24   c) 32   d) None of these.

Question 20

12	15	
*	45	162
108		486

a) 48   b) 40   c) 36   d) None of these.

Question 21

49	77	
43	71	164
*	65	158

a) 40   b) 38   c) 34   d) None of these.

Question 22

275	55	*
50	10	2
	15	3

a) 5   b) 11   c) 15   d) None of these.

Question 23

	3	18
2	6	*
4	12	72

a) 32　　　　　　b) 36　　　　　　c) 42　　　　　　d) None of these.

Question 24

If people spend two-thirds of their life awake, how many years would one spend sleeping if one lived to be 85 years old?

a) 24　　　　　　b) 26　　　　　　c) 28　　　　　　d) None of these.

Question 25

In an electronic sale, a television was reduced by one-third from the original price. What was the original price if the new sales price is $70?

a) $ 116　　　　　b) $ 105　　　　　c) $ 100　　　　　d) None of these.

Question 26

A travel agent is allowed to reserve 5 rooms at any one booking. How many bookings are required to reserve 16 rooms?

a) 3　　　　　　b) 5　　　　　　c) 7　　　　　　d) None of these.

Question 27

In a pizza eating contest a man can eat an eighth of his own weight in 45 minutes. If the man weighs 80 kg, how much can he eat in 30 minutes?

a) 5 1/3 kg　　　b) 5 2/3 kg　　　c) 6 1/3 kg　　　d) 6 2/3 kg

Question 28

Solve for "y"　　　$21 + 15 \times 5 - y + 14 = 88$

a) 22　　　　　　b) 25　　　　　　c) 18　　　　　　d) None of these.

Question 29

Solve for "y"　　　$y - 42 = 103$

a) 61　　　　　　b) 127　　　　　　c) 144　　　　　　d) None of these.

Question 30

Solve for "y"　　　$20 + y \times 2 - 28 + 14 = 30$

a) 8　　　　　　b) 12　　　　　　c) 14　　　　　　d) None of these.

Answer Key

Verbal

1) B
2) A
3) B
4) D
5) D
6) A
7) C
8) B
9) A
10) B
11) D
12) B
13) F
14) C
15) E

Spatial

1) B
2) A
3) A
4) D
5) A
6) A
7) C
8) B
9) A
10) C
11) D
12) B
13) A
14) A
15) B

16) C
17) B
18) B
19) B
20) A
21) B
22) A
23) D
24) B
25) C
26) B
27) D
28) D
29) C
30) B

31) A
32) A
33) C
34) C
35) C

Problem Solving

1) C
2) A
3) C
4) C
5) D
6) C
7) C
8) E
9) C
10) A
11) B
12) B
13) D
14) C
15) D

16) B
17) B
18) A
19) B
20) C
21) D
22) B
23) B
24) C
25) B
26) D
27) D
28) A
29) D
30) B

Verbal and Spatial tests – review the answer sheet.

Problem Solving Test

Question 1

521 x 346 = 180,266

Question 2

First subtract 4 hours from 1 pm, which brings you to 9 am. Then simply switch am to pm to subtract the remaining 12 hours. The answer is 9 pm.

Question 3

All of the products will cost a total of $42.24.

6 x $3.54 = $21.24   21.24 + 9.75 + 11.25 = 42.24

5 x $1.95 = $9.75

3 x $3.75 = $11.25

Then subtract the amount of the purchase from the dollars spent.

$50 – 42.24 = $7.76

Question 4

$\frac{15}{16}$ $\frac{7}{8}$ $\frac{3}{4}$ $\frac{2}{3}$ $\frac{1}{2}$ These fractions are all decreasing order. A sure way to check is to create a common denominator (48)

$\frac{45}{48}$ $\frac{42}{48}$ $\frac{36}{48}$ $\frac{32}{48}$ $\frac{24}{48}$

Question 5

The number of sides an object has keeps increasing by one.

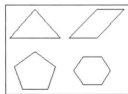

Question 6

Objects alternate between a circle and a circle with a cross (no colouring) on opposing corners.

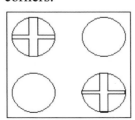

Question 7

Images from the first row are superimposed onto the second row, which results in the third row. Any overlap of small squares results in a colour change to black.

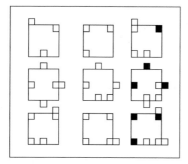

Question 8

The number of arrows is increasing by one each figure. The circles are internal on the bottom row and external on the top row.

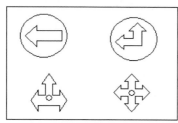

Question 9

The number of circles is decreasing by one and the number of squares is increasing by one.

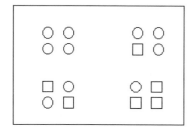

Question 10

The numbers are decreasing by 2 each time (33, 31, 29, 27, 25, 23...).

Question 11

The numbers are being multiplied by -2 (-4, 8, -16, 32, -64, 128, -256...).

Question 12

The numbers are being multiplied by 2 and added by 5 (2, 9, 23, 51, 107, ...).

Question 13

The numbers are decreasing by a factor of 1. (89, 88, 87, 86, 85, 84, 83...)

Question 14

The numbers are being multiplied by 2 and then subtracted by 3. (7, 11, 19, 35, 67, 131, 259...)

Question 15

The time between 1:45 pm and 3:30 pm is 1 and ¾ hours or 1:45 (3 2/4 – 1 ¾ = 1 ¾). You have to add another 12 hours for a total of 13 hours and 45 minutes (12:00 + 1:45 = 13:45).

Question 16

6 ½ = 6 2/4 = 26/4   3 ¾ = 15/4   4 ½ = 4 2/4 = 18/4

26 / 4 - 15 / 4 + 18 / 4 = 29 /4   =   7 ¼

Question 17

60 – 4 1/3 = 55 2/3 kg remain

Question 18

First determine what one-quarter of 32 is by dividing 32 by 4. 32 / 4 = 8. Next determine what number if doubled will give you 8. This is accomplished by dividing 8 by 2. The answer is 4 (8/2 = 4).

Question 19

Multiplying

	2	4
1	2	8
3	6	24
9	18	72

3 ↓

Question 20

Multiplying

12	15	27
36	45	162
108	135	486

3 ↓

Question 21

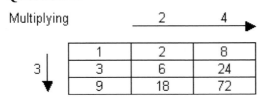

Adding

6 ↑

49	77	170
43	71	164
37	65	158

Question 22

Multiplying

5 ←

275	55	11
50	10	2
75	15	3

Question 23

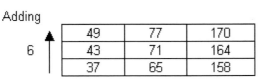

Multiplying

2 ↓

	3	6
1	3	18
2	6	36
4	12	72

Question 24

If a person spends two-thirds of their life awake, then they must spend 1/3 of their life asleep. All you have to do is divide 85 by 3. One would sleep 28 years (85 / 3 = 28.3).

Question 25

An algebraic equation is required to answer this question. Let "y" equal the original price. Therefore if you subtract 1/3 (y) from the product, the answer would be 70.

$$y - 1/3 (y) = 70$$

$$2/3 (y) = 70$$

$$y = 70 \div 2/3 \quad \text{(multiply by the reciprocal)} \quad y = 70 \times 3/2 = 210 / 2 = 105$$

The original price was $105.

Question 26

Simply divide 16 by 5 (16 / 5 = 3.2). Because in 3 bookings you could at most book 15 rooms, you will require 4 bookings to reserve 16 rooms.

Question 27

First determine how many kilograms he can eat in 45 minutes. 1/8 of 80 kg is 10 kg (80 / 8 = 10).

Next calculate how much he can eat in 30 minutes. 30 is 2/3 of 45, so in order to solve the problem, you have to multiply 2/3 and 10 kg (10 x 2/3 = 20/3 = 6.66 or 6 2/3 kg).

Question 28

$21 + 15 \times 5 - y + 14 = 88$

$21 + 75 - y + 14 = 88$

$96 - y + 14 - 14 = 88 - 14$

$96 - 96 - y = 74 - 96$

$-y = -22$

$y = 22$

Question 29

$y - 42 = 103$

$y - 42 + 42 = 103 + 42$

$y = 145$

Question 30

$20 + y \times 2 - 28 + 14 = 30$

$20 + y \times 2 - 14 = 30$

$20 + y \times 2 - 14 + 14 = 30 + 14$

$20 - 20 + y \times 2 = 44 - 20$

$y \times 2 = 24$

$y \times 2 / 2 = 24 / 2$

$y = 12$

Security Guard / Private Investigator Testing

The Licensing Test for both Security Guards and Private Investigators is a 60-question, multiple choice format written test. You should allow 2 hours for the entire test, although the maximum time allotted for completing it is 75 minutes. The test covers the following areas:

Security

1) Introduction to the Industry
2) Private Security Ministry Code of Conduct
3) Basic Security Procedures
4) Report Writing
5) Health & Safety
6) Emergency Response Preparation
7) Canadian Legal System
8) Legal Authorities
9) Effective Communications
10) Sensitivity Training
11) Use of Force Theory
12) Emergency First Aid

Private Investigation

1) Introduction to the Industry
2) The PSISA
3) Provincial and Federal Statutes
4) Criminal and Civil Law
5) Investigative Techniques
6) Principles of Ethical Reasoning
7) Communication and Interaction
8) Self-Management Skills

Only paper, pencils and erasers are allowed -- no books, dictionaries, notes, calculators, calculator watches or other aids are permitted in the room.

Detach the Answer Sheet to take the test.

	A B C D		A B C D		A B C D
1)	○ ○ ○ ○ ___	11)	○ ○ ○ ○ ___	21)	○ ○ ○ ○ ___
2)	○ ○ ○ ○ ___	12)	○ ○ ○ ○ ___	22)	○ ○ ○ ○ ___
3)	○ ○ ○ ○ ___	13)	○ ○ ○ ○ ___	23)	○ ○ ○ ○ ___
4)	○ ○ ○ ○ ___	14)	○ ○ ○ ○ ___	24)	○ ○ ○ ○ ___
5)	○ ○ ○ ○ ___	15)	○ ○ ○ ○ ___	25)	○ ○ ○ ○ ___
6)	○ ○ ○ ○ ___	16)	○ ○ ○ ○ ___	26)	○ ○ ○ ○ ___
7)	○ ○ ○ ○ ___	17)	○ ○ ○ ○ ___	27)	○ ○ ○ ○ ___
8)	○ ○ ○ ○ ___	18)	○ ○ ○ ○ ___	28)	○ ○ ○ ○ ___
9)	○ ○ ○ ○ ___	19)	○ ○ ○ ○ ___	29)	○ ○ ○ ○ ___
10)	○ ○ ○ ○ ___	20)	○ ○ ○ ○ ___	30)	○ ○ ○ ○ ___

	A B C D		A B C D		A B C D
31)	○ ○ ○ ○ ___	41)	○ ○ ○ ○ ___	51)	○ ○ ○ ○ ___
32)	○ ○ ○ ○ ___	42)	○ ○ ○ ○ ___	52)	○ ○ ○ ○ ___
33)	○ ○ ○ ○ ___	43)	○ ○ ○ ○ ___	53)	○ ○ ○ ○ ___
34)	○ ○ ○ ○ ___	44)	○ ○ ○ ○ ___	54)	○ ○ ○ ○ ___
35)	○ ○ ○ ○ ___	45)	○ ○ ○ ○ ___	55)	○ ○ ○ ○ ___
36)	○ ○ ○ ○ ___	46)	○ ○ ○ ○ ___	56)	○ ○ ○ ○ ___
37)	○ ○ ○ ○ ___	47)	○ ○ ○ ○ ___	57)	○ ○ ○ ○ ___
38)	○ ○ ○ ○ ___	48)	○ ○ ○ ○ ___	58)	○ ○ ○ ○ ___
39)	○ ○ ○ ○ ___	49)	○ ○ ○ ○ ___	59)	○ ○ ○ ○ ___
40)	○ ○ ○ ○ ___	50)	○ ○ ○ ○ ___	60)	○ ○ ○ ○ ___

Total ____ / 60

Security Guard Licensing Test 1

Question 1

Which of the following are basic duties of a security guard?

a) Patrolling sites and buildings and removing trespassers.

b) Securing evidence and making arrests.

c) Conducting crowd control and receiving lost property.

d) All of the above.

Question 2

Some federal statutes that may subject security guards to regulations, depending on where they work or their role, may include:

a) The Nuclear Safety Act and the Firearms Act.

b) The Canadian Air Transport Security Authority Act and the Firearms Act.

c) The National Energy Board Act and the Nuclear Safety Act.

d) All of the above.

Question 3

Which of the following would typically not be under the charge of private security guards?

a) People, property, and buildings.

b) Employers' interests, information, and assets.

c) Employers' reputations and local traffic laws such as seat belt violations.

d) Assets such as money or other valuable property.

Question 4

Which of the following are mandatory licensing requirements under the Private Security and Investigative Services Act, 2005?

a) Individuals must be 18 years of age.

b) Individuals must be entitled to work in Canada and have a clean criminal record.

c) Individuals must complete all prescribed training and testing.

d) All of the above.

Question 5

Which of the following would be something that security guards are prohibited from doing in their code of conduct?

a) Sleeping while on duty.

b) Working after consuming alcohol.

c) Using profane and insulting language.

d) All of the above.

Question 6

When applying for a security licence, a registrar may require an applicant to:

a) Provide fingerprints.

b) Provide personal medical records.

c) Provide a list of personal references.

d) All of the above.

Question 7

Which of the following would NOT be prohibited under the Private Security and Investigative Services Act?

a) Providing information to a client regarding the location of a person protected under a Witness Protection Program.

b) A person possessing both a Security Guard license and a Private Investigator License.

c) Obstructing an inspector conducting an inspection or destroying anything that is relevant to the inspection.

d) Failing to produce a licence while on duty at the request of a police officer.

Question 8

Which of the following are objectives of a patrol program?

a) To establish a presence to deter potential offenders.

b) To provide additional work to spare officers.

c) To prevent officers from resting when there are no activities to perform.

d) All of the above.

Question 9

Which of the following statements are true?

a) Security guards are permitted to direct traffic on public roadways in emergency situations.

b) Security guards are permitted to direct traffic on private property if they are acting in accordance with their duties.

c) Security guards are permitted to direct traffic on public road ways.

d) None of the above.

Question 10

Which of the following is the most important aspect of hand signals while directing pedestrian or vehicle traffic?

a) They be simple, consistent and clear.

b) They be clear and rhythmic to attract attention.

c) They be rhythmic and varied to prevent boredom.

d) All of the above.

Question 11

What is the primary purpose of a security guard uniform?

a) To display professionalism and a sense of authority so individuals will be more responsive to your presence.

b) To allow employees to perform their duties without damaging their own clothing.

c) To ensure that security guards have all the necessary equipment at their disposal.

d) All of the above.

Question 12

Which of the following are methods of ingesting illegal drugs?

a) Orally.

b) Snorting.

c) Smoking.

d) All of the above.

Question 13

Which of the following would be an example of an anomaly a security guard should be able to detect?

a) A cashier -- who normally leaves work early -- works late and remains behind after all other cashiers have left for the evening.

b) A fellow security guard who fails to take a scheduled break and is seen in an area outside of his regular patrol area.

c) A security camera by an entrance that has been repositioned to obscure the view.

d) All of the above.

Question 14

Which of the following are examples of questions that may need to be answered in a notebook?

a) Who interviewed the witness?

b) What damages were done?

c) When was the victim taken to the hospital?

d) All of the above.

Question 15

Which of the following characteristics are mandatory for every security guard's notebook?

a) Your notebook should have your name and contact information in it.

b) Your notebook should not have pages ripped out of it.

c) Dates should be included for all shifts and entries made.

d) All of the above.

Question 16

Which of the following actions should NOT be taken regarding a security guard's notebook?

a) Waiting before making notes due to a potential danger that needs to be addressed first.

b) Crossing out an error and initialling it to indicate that you corrected the error.

c) Ripping out a page where a serious error was made.

d) All of the above.

Question 17

Which of the following is true regarding the Occupational Health and Safety Act?

a) Responsibilities and duties are outlined for employers and employees in the regulation.

b) Responsibilities and duties are outlined for employees only.

c) Violations of the act can only occur for employers and owners.

d) According to the regulation, the condition of the workplace equipment is the responsibility of the employee.

Question 18

The key elements of the WHMIS system are:

a) Cautionary labelling of containers as WHMIS "controlled products."

b) Worker education programs.

c) The provision of Material Safety Data Sheets (MSDSs).

d) All of the above.

Question 19

Which of the following receives the lowest priority when approaching a crime scene?

a) Personal safety.

b) Permitting pedestrian and vehicle traffic to move without obstruction.

c) Noting and preserving evidence.

d) Ensuring people receive appropriate first aid treatment.

Question 20

Which of the following are methods that should be used to preserve evidence at a crime scene?

a) If there is a victim, make a sketch in your notebook noting the position where they were found.

b) If it is necessary, create a safe walkway through a crime scene.

c) Park a vehicle over shoe prints in the snow to ensure that no one else steps on them.

d) All of the above.

Question 21

Which of the following are tools security guards can use to help secure evidence at a crime scene?

a) Pylons and obstruction barriers.

b) Caution tape.

c) Video and digital cameras.

d) All of the above.

Question 22

Which of the following must be prioritized when managing an emergency scene?

a) Ensuring people receive appropriate first aid treatment.

b) Permitting pedestrian and vehicle traffic to move by opening up the scene.

c) Noting and preserving evidence.

d) All of the above.

Question 23

Security receives a letter in the mail claiming there is a poisonous substance in the envelope. However, there are no signs of this powder or any other substance on the envelope. Which actions are appropriate?

a) You can ignore the envelope as it is probably a hoax.

b) You should contact the police immediately, and leave the envelope in a secure area under guard.

c) You should open the envelope. If there is any sign of a suspicious substance you should contact police immediately.

d) All of the above.

Question 24

Which of the following tools or pieces of equipment would be important to the police at a crime scene investigation?

a) Security videos of the area being investigated.

b) Log reports of people who had access to the area.

c) Incident reports of suspicious activity recently in the crime scene area?

d) All of the above.

Question 25

Where would the authority to search an arrested subject for evidence, or implements to inflict injury or aid escape, come from?

a) Common Law.

b) Civil Law.

c) Statute Law.

d) All of the above.

Question 26

Which of the following are rights guaranteed under the Charter of Rights and Freedoms?

a) Individuals have a right to receive advice from counsel upon arrest.

b) Individuals cannot be tried twice for the same crime.

c) Individuals are guaranteed bail except in cases of murder.

d) All of the above.

Question 27

What is the best definition of the term "Colour of Right?"

a) An honest belief in entitlement.

b) A belief that you will not be caught in the act.

c) A belief that a law is immoral, and so shouldn't be followed.

d) All of the above.

Question 28

What is a summary conviction offence?

a) A less serious offence, such as causing a disturbance.

b) A municipal by-law, such as a noise violation.

c) A provincial offence, such as a violation of the Liquor Licence Act.

d) All of the above.

Question 29

Which of the following is a set of facts or circumstances which would lead an ordinary reasonable person to a belief beyond a mere suspicion.

a) Facts in Issue.

b) Relevant Evidence.

c) Reasonable Grounds.

d) None of the above.

Question 30

What are the three forms of evidence?

a) Physical, hearsay, and inadmissible.

b) Hearsay, admissible, and prohibited.

c) Real, testimony, and documentary.

d) None of the above.

Question 31

Which of the following are common municipal by-laws that a security guard should be familiar with?

a) Noise by-laws.

b) Occupancy limits.

c) Parking by-laws.

d) All of the above.

Question 32

Which of the following must be done to affect an arrest?

a) Gain physical control of a person and inform them that they are under arrest.

b) Taking physical control of a person without informing them that they are under arrest is sufficient.

c) Send an appearance notice requiring a person to attend court to a person's home.

d) All of the above.

Question 33

Which of the following statements regarding witnesses to a breach of the peace are true?

a) Only police officers may detain people they witness breaching the peace.

b) Police officers may not receive into custody any person handed over to them from a private citizen for a breach of the peace.

c) Any person who witnesses a breach of the peace is justified in interfering to prevent its continuance and may detain the offender in order to transfer him to the custody of a peace officer.

d) Both options A and B are correct.

Question 34

Which of the following are purposes of the Labour Relations Act, 1995?

a) To promote flexibility, productivity, and employee involvement in the workplace.

b) To encourage communication between employers and employees in the workplace.

c) To facilitate collective bargaining between employers and the trade unions that are the freely-designated representatives of the employees.

d) All of the above.

Question 35

Which of the following areas are covered under the Employment Standards Act?

a) Payment of Wages.

b) Hours of Work and Eating Periods.

c) Overtime Pay and Public Holidays.

d) All of the above.

Question 36

Which of the following are elements in the offence of mischief?

a) Wilfully destroying or damaging property.

b) Rendering property dangerous, useless, inoperative, or ineffective.

c) Obstructing, interrupting or interfering with the lawful use, enjoyment, or operation of property.

d) All of the above.

Question 37

What are the two elements necessary to justify a charge of possessing property obtained by an indictable offence?

a) 1) Have knowledge of the whereabouts of a property or thing; 2) The thing has to have been stolen or obtained by an indictable offence (or what would be an indictable offence if committed outside Canada).

b) 1) Have possession of property or a thing; 2) Have knowledge it was obtained by an indictable offence (or what would be an indictable offence if committed outside Canada).

c) 1) Have possession of property or a thing; 2) The thing has to have been stolen, or obtained by an indictable offence (or what would be an indictable offence if committed outside Canada).

d) None of the above.

Question 38

Which of the following are NOT listed as actions in the offence of Cause Disturbance?

a) Having sex in a public place.

b) Singing.

c) Swearing.

d) None of the above.

Question 39

In situations where self-defence is required, which of the following is true?

a) You are authorized to use force to defend yourself in an unprovoked attack.

b) You are authorized to use lethal force if reasonable grounds exist that your life is in danger.

c) You are allowed to use force to defend yourself when you are preventing an assault.

d) All of the above.

Question 40

Which of the following is the best definition of Tort Law?

a) A body of law that addresses and provides remedies for civil wrongs not arising out of contractual obligations (such as accidents, negligence, and libel).

b) Any law involving the settling private contractual disputes between citizens.

c) A body of law that allows citizens to seek remedy from people in authority.

d) All of the above.

Question 41

A security guard in the employ of a store is informed that someone stole a camera and left the store. The guard follows the person of interest out of the store and arrests him or her in the parking lot. Which of the following is true?

a) The arrest was lawful because the security guard witnessed a person committing a provincial offence against the property they are protecting.

b) The arrest was unlawful because the security guard did not witness the person committing the act.

c) The arrest was unlawful because the agent did not arrest the person on the store property and has no authority to arrest a person outside of the property they are protecting.

d) The arrest was lawful because the security guard is an authorized agent of the store, there was a criminal offence made against the property of the store, and the arrested person was found committing the criminal offence.

Question 42

Which of the following would be considered personal information under the Personal Information Protection and Electronic Documents Act?

a) Age, name, ID numbers, income, ethnic origin, or blood type.

b) Employee files, credit records, loan records, medical records, existence of a dispute between a consumer and a merchant, and intentions.

c) Opinions, evaluations, comments, social status, or disciplinary actions.

d) All of the above.

Question 43

You are a security guard working in a high school. You have received complaints that a man on the school grounds had been told several times to leave by the principal and is refusing to do so. You find the man just outside of the school grounds. There is a police officer in the area as well. What action can be taken?

a) You can ask the police officer to issue a ticket to the man for trespassing. The police officer will be able to arrest the male if he refuses to identify himself.

b) With the assistance of the police officer, you can arrest the male for trespassing, even if the man provides his name and address.

c) You can arrest the male for trespassing (failing to leave when asked/told to do so) and turn him over to the police officer immediately.

d) All of the above.

Question 44

What questions are important to answer when filling out written reports?

a) Who? & When?

b) What? & Why?

c) Where? & How?

d) All of the above.

Question 45

Which of the following principles are important to assist you in increasing your essential listening skills?

a) Keeping your mind open, resisting distractions, and listening for ideas.

b) Making assumptions based on your personal experience and controlling the speed of the dialogue.

c) Finishing other persons' sentences to indicate your understanding, and actively monitoring your surroundings while listening to a statement.

d) All of the above.

Question 46

You encounter an angry individual who is venting. What is an effective step in de-escalation?

a) Remaining calm and allowing the person to vent for a couple of seconds before intervening.

b) Taking control of the situation by telling them to stop immediately.

c) Shouting loudly to distract the person and shock them into calming down.

d) All of the above.

Question 47

Which of the following actions would be an effective method of dealing with a woman panhandling in front of the building you are responsible for patrolling?

a) Assessing the problem and finding out if the woman is hungry and homeless.

b) Arresting the woman for repeated trespassing, removing her daily, giving her money or food, or directing her towards a shelter and soup kitchen.

c) Informing her of the location of a soup kitchen and shelter, and cautioning her that she may be arrested for trespassing if her behaviour continues.

d) All of the above.

Question 48

Which of the following would make a report prepared by a security guard seem unprofessional?

a) A hand-written report that is illegible.

b) Grammar and spelling mistakes throughout the report.

c) A report that contains a racial stereotype.

d) All of the above.

Question 49

Which of the following should be considered when dealing with a person you suspect has a mental illness?

a) Realizing that it is your job to contact their families or a doctor to look after them.

b) Realizing that they might not be able to take care of themselves and may need support or assistance.

c) Realizing that the police should be contacted whenever you encounter a person you suspect has a mental illness.

d) All of the above.

Question 50

You are in charge of the company barbeque. Because one of your co-workers is a vegetarian, you should:

a) Disregard him, as he can bring his own food to the barbeque.

b) Give him a regular hamburger and tell him it's vegetarian.

c) Tell him it's unfair to expect special meals be made for him.

d) None of the above.

Question 51

Which of the following steps would be most appropriate when you are taking a statement from a person whose accent is difficult to understand?

a) Continue taking the information down as best you can without expressing your difficulty.

b) Ask the person to please speak slower, explaining that you are having difficulty understanding them.

c) Ask the person to attempt to speak without the accent.

d) All of the above.

Question 52

One of your co-workers continuously tells sexist jokes while on the job. He only does this when there are men around. You know other co-workers have told him on several occasions that his jokes are inappropriate. What is the best course of action?

a) Ignore the jokes, as no one is hurt because there are only men are around.

b) Inform a supervisor that the co-worker is telling sexist jokes.

c) Let him know that you feel the jokes are inappropriate.

d) All of the above.

Question 53

What is an Impact Factor?

a) An excuse used to justify the excessive use of force in the course of regular duties.

b) A condition unique to a person and situation which will affect which decision is made while responding with force.

c) A justification for any use of force under any condition.

d) All of the above.

Question 54

Which of the following statements is true regarding the Use of Force Response Options?

a) Tactical communication is appropriate to use during all threat levels (compliance, serious bodily harm, and threat).

b) Empty hand techniques can mean restraining techniques, joint locks, punching, and grounding techniques.

c) Impact weapons can include both strikes and blocks.

d) All of the above.

Question 55

Which of the following would help prevent positional asphyxia?

a) Drunkenness.

b) Physical disability.

c) Restraint.

d) None of the above.

Question 56

Which of the following must be considered when assessing an emergency scene?

a) Determining if you have enough time to begin working on a scene before your shift ends.

b) Getting assistance from other security guards, police officers, fire fighters, paramedics, tow trucks drivers, or any other service required.

c) Tending to the injuries of emergency service personnel before any other victims or suspects.

d) All of the above.

Question 57

From a First Aid or CPR perspective, which of the following statements is true regarding unconsciousness?

a) A sleeping person will respond to loud noises or gentle shaking, but an unconscious person will not.

b) Unconsciousness is only a concern if the person is diabetic.

c) An unconscious person can cough and clear their throat if they need to.

d) Unconsciousness by itself is not a medical emergency.

Question 58

At what point should you cease performing the Heimlich manoeuvre?

a) After five thrusts, at which point reassess the victim.

b) Until the victim indicates they are fine by grabbing their throat.

c) Until the object is expelled or until the person loses consciousness.

d) All of the above.

Question 59

Which of the following could be a cause of severe bleeding?

a) Haemophilia, leukemia, and cancer.

b) Tooth Extraction.

c) Certain medications.

d) All of the above.

Question 60

What is the best way to activate the emergency medical system when you are required to perform CPR?

a) Inform someone they are responsible for activating the emergency medical system, and inform them of the status of the patient so they can pass this information on to the operator.

b) Advise several people to contact the emergency medical system. Inform them of the status of the patient so they can pass the information on to the operator.

c) Cease what you are doing and contact the emergency medical system personally as you are the most aware of what is wrong with the patient.

d) Focus your efforts on the patient and allow someone else to worry about calling for help and activating the emergency medical system.

1) D	16) C	31) D	46) A
2) D	17) A	32) A	47) D
3) C	18) D	33) C	48) D
4) D	19) B	34) D	49) B
5) D	20) A	35) D	50) D
6) A	21) D	36) D	51) B
7) B	22) D	37) B	52) B
8) A	23) B	38) A	53) B
9) B	24) D	39) D	54) D
10) A	25) A	40) A	55) D
11) A	26) A	41) B	56) B
12) D	27) A	42) D	57) A
13) D	28) A	43) A	58) C
14) D	29) C	44) D	59) D
15) D	30) C	45) A	60) A

Detailed Answers

Question 1

The duties of security guards include all of the above and more: maintaining logs, enforcing rules, directing traffic, responding to incidents, assisting police, providing first aid, and CPR.

Question 2

Other federal statutes that may subject security guards to regulation include: the Aeronautics Act, the National Energy Board Act, the Firearms Act, the Canadian Air Transport Security Authority Act, and the Nuclear Safety Act.

Question 3

Security guards would not be responsible for enforcing highway traffic act violations. These are the responsibilities of the police.

Question 4

Requirements include: a clean criminal record, being the minimum age of 18, the legal entitlement to work in Canada, and having successfully completed all required training and testing.

Question 5

Security guard codes of conduct often prohibit profane language, making false statements, conducting personal business while on duty, abusing power, failing to carry out assigned duties, and sleeping while on duty.

Question 6

Registrars may require any of the following from applicants: fingerprints, a photograph, consent to have the police perform a background check, consent to investigate the applicant's immigration status, or any other information considered necessary to determine if an applicant meets the requirements for the issuance or renewal of a license.

Question 7

A person is permitted to possess both licenses, but may not act as both a security guard and a private investigator at the same time.

Question 8

The objectives of patrol programs include: gaining knowledge of a site, investigating any situations that affect the normal routine of the site, detecting crimes, building confidence about security in the minds of employees, management and/or residents, and establishing a visible presence to deter potential offenders.

Question 9

The Highway Traffic Act, which governs who is allowed to direct traffic, applies to roadways. Security guards are allowed to direct traffic on private property.

Question 10

Hand signals used in directing traffic have to be consistent, clear, and simple. Drivers need to know exactly what you want them to do. Any confusion in your manual commands could result in collisions and injuries.

Question 11

Professional uniforms worn by security guards and police officers instil a sense of authority. They provide the wearers an advantage when performing their duties.

Question 12

Security guards may come across debris from syringes and pipes that may pose a danger to them. Forms of ingestion include oral, snorting, smoking, sublingual (under the tongue), and intravenous (through needles).

Question 13

These are all examples of anomalies that a security guard should be able to notice and either take note of it for future use, or immediately act on if the situation warrants it.

Question 14

The more detailed the notes the better. Your notebook should basically answer the simple questions of Who? What? Where? When? How? And, if possible, Why? The more of these questions that are answered by your notes, the better the notes are.

Question 15

It is important to identify your notebook as it is your property and responsibility. Pages should not be ripped out and all of your entries should be dated.

Question 16

Notes need to be taken while the event is still fresh in your mind, but they do not have to be made instantaneously. Any dangerous situations should be dealt with first. Errors should be crossed off and initialled in such a way that the original writing can still be read. It is inappropriate to rip out pages from a notebook, which can lead to accusations of dishonesty.

Question 17

Responsibilities and duties are outlined for employers and employees in the regulation. Both employers and employees can violate the act. Equipment is the responsibility of both the employers and the employees.

Question 18

WHMIS is the Workplace Hazardous Materials Information System. The key elements of the system are cautionary labelling of containers of WHMIS "controlled products," the provision of material safety data sheets (MSDSs), and worker education programs.

Question 19

The very last thing you do on a crime scene is open it up to pedestrian and vehicle traffic. Personal safety is first, followed by preservation of life, protection of property, and securing evidence. It is a good idea to have preserving evidence in mind while performing your duties, but not at the expense of increasing danger, or risking life or further property damage.

Question 20

It is important to make notes at a crime scene, especially regarding evidence that might have to be moved or manipulated, such as a victim who may require CPR or transfer to a hospital. A crime scene perimeter is more important than satisfying pedestrian concerns and should be respected. Driving a vehicle over top of shoe prints in the snow would likely melt them and should not be done.

Question 21

Pylons, obstruction barriers, and cautionary tape can be used to set up a perimeter or cordon off important areas which will be investigated. Pictures and videos could be vital pieces of evidence that can be taken prior to moving any objects.

Question 22

The very last thing you do on a crime scene is open it up to pedestrian and vehicle traffic. Personal safety is first, followed by preservation of life, protection of property, and securing evidence. It is a good idea to have preserving evidence in mind while performing your duties, but not at the expense of increasing danger, or risking life or further property damage.

Question 23

A letter containing no visible powder and a threatening note needs to be reported to authorities so that a HAZMAT unit can be dispatched. There could be trace amounts of poison that may pose a risk.

Question 24

Police would be interested in all of the above materials at a crime scene. They all may provide evidence or clues that would need to be followed up.

Question 25

Common Laws are laws accepted as a matter of custom and tradition. They include the right of Peace Officers to search a person in lawful custody and to remove from such persons articles of evidence, injury, and escape.

Question 26

Individuals have a right to receive advice from counsel upon arrest. In Canada a person can be tried twice for the same crime. Double Jeopardy is an American concept. Individuals aren't guaranteed bail. For some offences and in many circumstances they may be denied bail.

Question 27

Colour of Right refers to an honest belief of entitlement. An example of this might occur when a person who is accused of stealing a bag honestly believes they were picking up their own bag and didn't mean to take someone else's.

Question 28

Summary conviction offences are less serious federal offences. Provincial and municipal offences are not criminal acts.

Question 29

Reasonable grounds is a set of facts or circumstances which can lead a reasonable person to a belief beyond a mere suspicion. Facts in issue is the information leading to a charge answering who, what, where and when.

Question 30

Real evidence is physical evidence that can be seen, felt, touched, or experienced. Testimony is the evidence presented verbally by witnesses or parties to an offence or issue. Documentary evidence are forms, files, logs, or other recordings indicating transactions or movements of people and things.

Question 31

Municipal by-laws will vary between municipalities. You will have to make sure you review and become familiar with any relevant by-laws in the area where you are working.

Question 32

In order for an arrest to be legal, the person placing someone under arrest must take physical control and inform the person that they are under arrest. This is usually done by touching a person in an attempt to get physical control. However, simply stating the words can also constitute an arrest.

Question 33

Everyone who witnesses a breach of the peace is justified in interfering to prevent the continuance of this breach. They may detain the person committing the offence to transfer him into the custody of a peace officer. Peace officers can receive into custody any person who may have been a party to a breach of the peace by someone who the officer believes on reasonable grounds witnessed this breach of peace.

Question 34

The purposes of the Labour Relations Act are: 1) To facilitate collective bargaining between employers and the trade unions that are the freely-designated representatives of the employees. 2) To recognize the importance of workplace parties adapting to change. 3) To promote flexibility, productivity, and employee involvement in the workplace. 4) To encourage communication between employers and employees in the workplace. 5) To recognize the importance of economic growth as the foundation for mutually beneficial relations amongst employers, employees, and trade unions. 6) To encourage co-operative participation of employers and trade unions in resolving workplace issues. 7) To promote the expeditious resolution of workplace disputes.

Question 35

Employment standards are enforced under the Employment Standards Act, 2000 (ESA), which sets out the minimum standards that employers and employees must follow.

Question 36

The sections concerning Mischief include: 1) Wilfully destroying or damaging property. 2) Rendering property dangerous, useless, inoperative or ineffective. 3) Obstructing, interrupting or interfering with the lawful use, enjoyment, or operation of the property. 4) Obstructing, interrupting, or interfering with any person in the lawful use, enjoyment, or operation of the property.

Question 37

The two elements necessary to justify a charge of possessing property obtained by indictable offence are: 1) Having possession of property or a thing. 2) Having knowledge it was obtained by an indictable offence (or what would be an indictable offence if the crime was committed outside Canada). A person must have knowledge that the item is illegal.

Question 38

The elements of Cause Disturbance are: fighting, screaming, shouting, swearing, singing, insulting language, obscene language, being drunk, impeding other persons, and molesting other persons. Other actions that can apply include discharging a firearm, loitering or exposing an indecent exhibition in a public place. Dwelling houses, and people living in apartment buildings, are not subject to the offence. Courts may draw an inference from the evidence of a peace officer that a disturbance occurred. Witnesses are not always required, but may help a case.

Question 39

In defence of property you are authorized to use force to defend yourself. Lethal force is authorized if reasonable grounds exist that your life is in danger.

Question 40

Tort Law is a body of law that addresses and provides remedies for civil wrongs not arising out of contractual obligations.

Question 41

The arrest was unlawful because the security guard did not witness the person committing the act. The customer, who is not an agent of the property, found the person committing the criminal act.

Question 42

Personal information includes any factual or subjective information, recorded or not, about an identifiable individual. This includes information in any form, such as: 1) Age, name, ID numbers, income, ethnic origin or blood type. 2) Opinions, evaluations, comments, social status, or disciplinary actions. 3) Employee files, credit records, loan records, medical records, existence of a dispute between a consumer and a merchant, intentions (for example, to acquire goods or services, or change jobs). Personal information does not include the name, title, business address or telephone number of an employee of an organization.

Question 43

Only police officers can arrest the person if they freshly departed the property AND they fail to identify themselves. A security guard cannot arrest the person unless they find the suspect committing the offence.

Question 44

Security reports should cover all of the basic questions of an event including Who, What, Where, When, How and, if possible, Why.

Question 45

There are a number of principles that can aid in increasing essential listening skills. They include: keeping your mind open, resisting distractions, and listening for ideas. It is best to focus on the speaker when actively listening to them, and not interrupt their statements. It is also advisable to keep an open mind than to bring your own assumptions into the conversation.

Question 46

Timed Verbal Intervention (TVI) recognizes that people cannot vent indefinitely. They have to stop and catch their breath every 12 - 18 seconds. A good strategy is to remain calm and wait for the strategic moment to intervene.

Question 47

All of the above steps are effective uses of the TAGS strategy. Other options include finding out about her family and asking her if she would like help contacting them.

Question 48

All of the instances mentioned would make a report written by a security guard appear unprofessional.

Question 49

People with mental illness often have difficulty looking after themselves. If you are able to provide some assistance to them in the course of your duties, it may solve a long-term problem for both them and your organization. Security guards do not have any special power or authority when they encounter people with apparent mental disorders.

Question 50

The best action would be to simply arrange to have a couple of vegetarian burgers made for anyone who is a vegetarian.

Question 51

You will be encountering people with many different accents from many different backgrounds. There is nothing wrong with politely asking a person to slow down so you can understand them better. It is better to do this than fail to get all of the relevant information. It would be inappropriate and disrespectful to ask a person not to speak with an accent.

Question 52

It would be inappropriate to ignore the situation. Despite the fact that there are no women around, people can be hurt in work environments in which co-workers are disrespectful of others. The person has already been warned by other co-workers, to no apparent effect. At this stage, informing a supervisor would be appropriate.

Question 53

An Impact Factor is a condition unique to a person and situation which will affect what decision is made while responding with force. Impact Factors that may affect a persons' choice on the Use of Force response include: size, strength, personal experience, skills, abilities, fears, perceptions, and gender. Impact Factors will not justify any action at any level of resistance.

Question 54

All of the statements are true. Tactical communication is appropriate to use during all threat levels (compliance, serious bodily harm, and threat). Empty hand techniques can mean restraining techniques, joint locks, punching, and grounding techniques. Impact weapons can include both strikes and blocks.

Question 55

Positional asphyxia is the positioning of the body in a manner where it interferes with breathing. This can be a dangerous situation when a person is under arrest because it can lead to death. Drunkenness, physical disability, restraint, entrapment, and head injuries are all hazards which contribute to positional asphyxia.

Question 56

It is important to notify and get the proper support to assist you in dealing with any emergency situation. Concern for the end of your shift should not be a factor in your decision-making in these types of events. When treating injuries, there may be victims, or even suspects, that require medical care ahead of emergency service personnel, depending on the natures of the injuries.

Question 57

Unconsciousness is when a person is unable to respond to people and activities. Often this is called a coma, or being in a comatose state. Other changes in awareness can occur without becoming unconscious. Medically, these are called "altered mental status" or "changed mental status." They include sudden confusion, disorientation, or stupor. Unconsciousness or any other sudden change in mental status must be treated as a medical emergency. Being asleep is not the same thing as being unconscious. A sleeping person will respond to loud noises or gentle shaking. An unconscious person will not. An unconscious person cannot cough or clear his or her throat. This can lead to death if the airway becomes blocked.

Question 58

A series of thrusts should be repeated until the object is expelled. If the person loses consciousness, the rescuer should stop the thrusts. Steps should be taken to open the airway and provide artificial respiration. Failure of the chest to rise indicates that the airway is still blocked. The rescuer should then check the airway for and remove any visible objects. Artificial respiration should then be resumed.

Question 59

Causes of severe bleeding may include: accidents/falls, a blow to the head, injuries like scalp wounds, tooth extraction, certain medications and illnesses such as Haemophilia,

Scurvy, Cancer, Thrombocytopenia, A-plastic Anaemia, Leukemia, Haemorrhage, Peptic Ulcer, Platelet Disorder, Liver Disease, or Septicaemia.

Question 60

Inform someone they are responsible for activating the emergency medical system, and inform them of the status of the patient so they can pass this information on to the operator. Studies have shown when one person takes personal responsibility for an act it is more likely to be accomplished. If multiple people are asked, they will avoid the responsibility and assume someone else will perform the task.

Answer Sheet Private Investigator Licencing Test

A B C D
1) ○○○○ ___
2) ○○○○ ___
3) ○○○○ ___
4) ○○○○ ___
5) ○○○○ ___
6) ○○○○ ___
7) ○○○○ ___
8) ○○○○ ___
9) ○○○○ ___
10) ○○○○ ___

A B C D
11) ○○○○ ___
12) ○○○○ ___
13) ○○○○ ___
14) ○○○○ ___
15) ○○○○ ___
16) ○○○○ ___
17) ○○○○ ___
18) ○○○○ ___
19) ○○○○ ___
20) ○○○○ ___

A B C D
21) ○○○○ ___
22) ○○○○ ___
23) ○○○○ ___
24) ○○○○ ___
25) ○○○○ ___
26) ○○○○ ___
27) ○○○○ ___
28) ○○○○ ___
29) ○○○○ ___
30) ○○○○ ___

A B C D
31) ○○○○ ___
32) ○○○○ ___
33) ○○○○ ___
34) ○○○○ ___
35) ○○○○ ___
36) ○○○○ ___
37) ○○○○ ___
38) ○○○○ ___
39) ○○○○ ___
40) ○○○○ ___

A B C D
41) ○○○○ ___
42) ○○○○ ___
43) ○○○○ ___
44) ○○○○ ___
45) ○○○○ ___
46) ○○○○ ___
47) ○○○○ ___
48) ○○○○ ___
49) ○○○○ ___
50) ○○○○ ___

A B C D
51) ○○○○ ___
52) ○○○○ ___
53) ○○○○ ___
54) ○○○○ ___
55) ○○○○ ___
56) ○○○○ ___
57) ○○○○ ___
58) ○○○○ ___
59) ○○○○ ___
60) ○○○○ ___

Total ___ / 60

Private Investigator Licensing Test

Question 1

When did the PSISA come into force?

a) 2005   b) 2000   c) It has not taken effect   d) None of the above

Question 2

Which of the following statements is true?

a) All private investigators must fulfill mandatory requirements of the Training and Testing Regulation in order to be eligible to apply for a licence.

b) Private investigators must fulfill mandatory requirements of the Training and Testing Regulation only after they are hired.

c) In order to be granted a Private Investigators licence, you only need to pass a written test.

d) Private Investigators can operate as such if they have a Private Security Licence as both industries are covered by the same legislation.

Question 3

Which of the following conditions have to be met in order to require a private investigators licence?

a) Receive some form of payment or compensation.

b) Conduct investigations.

c) Areas focused on actions, business, occupation, whereabouts of a person or character.

d) All of the above are required.

Question 4

Which of the following are requirements in order to be eligible for a private investigator licence?

a) Be at least 18 years old.

b) Never been charged with a crime.

c) Be a Canadian Citizen.

d) None of the above.

Question 5

Which of the following is a violation of the PSISA?

a) Referring to themselves as a "Private Detective".

b) Referring to themselves as an "Officer".

c) Referring to themselves as a "Specialist".

d) None of the above.

PublicServicePrep.com   211

Question 6

Which of the following convictions without pardons would prevent an application from being accepted?

a) A person convicted of aggravated assault.

b) A person convicted of Forgery.

c) A person convicted of assault.

d) Both A and B.

Question 7

Which of the following statements is true?

a) The PSISA does not have any punitive measures against violators of the act.

b) The PSISA only has the power to fine violators.

c) The PSISA has the ability to fine a violator of the act up to $25,000 and / or imprison a violator for up to a year.

d) None of the above.

Question 8

What act governs the collection, use and disclosure of personal information by commercial organizations?

a) PIPEDA   b) PSISA

c) PSISB   d) All of the above.

Question 9

Which of the following circumstances would not require consent for the collection of personal information?

a) Publicly available records.

b) During some investigations of breaches of agreements.

c) During some investigations of contraventions of a law.

d) All of the above.

Question 10

What is important for Private Investigators to be aware of regarding FIPPA and MFIPPA?

a) They should know how to circumvent the laws to get access to the information they are after.

b) They should avoid any information controlled by agencies affected by the legislation.

c) They should know how to file access requests for records subject to the acts.

d) None of the above.

Question 11

Which of the following places would most likely be considered a reasonable expectation of privacy?

a) An individual watching television at home in their living room with the blinds open.

b) An individual barbequing on their balcony of their apartment.

c) An individual in their bedroom with their blinds partially closed.

d) An individual reading on their front porch.

Question 12

Which of the following concerns should private investigators have regarding filming individuals actions?

a) Not altering the original recording in any way.

b) Recording private conversations without audio.

c) Both of the above.

d) None of the above.

Question 13

Which of the following is a condition where an individual is permitted to record a private conversation under section 184 of the Criminal Code?

a) When the conversation took place in a public place.

b) When the individuals are being recorded with audio devices only.

c) Where there is consent granted from the originator or intended receiver of the message.

d) All of the above.

Question 14

Which of the following would be an acceptable situation for using a GPS tracking device?

a) Using a GPS on a subject's vehicle at the request of a girlfriend who suspects infidelity.

b) A business owner provides permission to use such a device on a company vehicle.

c) Using a GPS on a government vehicle to track a government employee you are privately investigating.

d) Both B and C.

Question 15

Which of the following would be an example of circumstantial evidence?

a) A robbery suspect being in the immediate area at the time a robbery occurred.

b) A witness stating they saw an individual strike a victim and steal a wallet.

c) A video recording of the actual circumstance of the robbery.

d) Both A and C.

Question 16

Documentary Evidence:

a) is any written thing capable of being made evidence.

b) may include books, photos or video tapes.

c) may include computer records or other information recorded or stored by means of any device.

d) All of the above.

Question 17

A knife found by a private investigator at the scene of a murder and presented in court would be an example of:

a) Real evidence

b) Trace evidence

c) Documentary evidence

d) Compelling evidence

Question 18

What is not required for opinion evidence to be admissible in court?

a) Opinion must be based on facts that have already been received in evidence.

b) Opinions have to come from experts who can provide an educated or professional opinion on the presented evidence.

c) The defense must stipulate that the individual providing the opinion evidence is in fact an expert.

d) None of the above.

Question 19

Which of the following statements is false according to the Trespass to Property Act?

a) If an arrest is made, police must be contacted as soon as possible.

b) A person entering a location where entry is prohibited and has been notified of this may be arrested.

c) If open to the public, individuals cannot be asked to leave.

d) None of the above.

Question 20

Which of the following statements is true?

a) Powers of arrest for private investigators would be authorized under the Criminal Code of Canada.

b) Private Investigators have additional arrest powers, which normal citizens do not possess.

c) If an arrest is made, a private investigator will always have to appear in court to justify and explain the arrest.

d) None of the above.

Question 21

Which of the following situations would allow a person to make a citizen's arrest?

a) If they believe an individual is wanted on a warrant regarding an offence where they were the victim and it is not practical to await the police.

b) If they witness a criminal offence being committed.

c) If they believe a criminal offence may be committed which may result in bodily harm.

d) None of the above.

Question 22

In which of the following situations would a person not be allowed to make a citizen's arrest?

a) If they are the immediate victim to a serious criminal offence.

b) If they witness an indictable offence being committed.

c) If they believe a criminal offence may be committed which may result in bodily harm.

d) All of the above.

Question 23

Which of the following is true regarding an arrest made by a Private Investigator?

a) They must notify police prior to making an arrest and deliver the individual arrested to a peace officer as soon as possible.

b) They may use force to affect an arrest.

c) They must provide an arrested person their rights to counsel.

d) All of the above.

Question 24

Which of the following are concerns a private investigator may have if too much force is used during an arrest?

a) Criminal Prosecution

b) Civil Litigation

c) Personal or public injury

d) All of the above.

Question 25

What conditions are required to use force on a person to prevent the commission of an offence?

a) The offence must be one where the perpetrator could be arrested under provincial legislation.

b) The offence could cause serious injury to a person.

c) The offence could cause public disdain.

d) All of the above.

Question 26

Which of the following are requirements a private investigator should be prepared for regarding the Canadian Criminal Court System?

a) Presenting evidence to the courts.

b) Preparing Crown Briefs and keeping courts informed of the status of cases.

c) Instructing witnesses how best to testify and what evidence to include / ignore.

d) All of the above.

Question 27

Which of the following assumptions / actions would be useful for a private investigator to make / take during the course of each investigation?

a) Assuming every investigation could lead to a trial.

b) Administrative and procedural requirements should be handled with the utmost care.

c) Key witnesses should be kept track of and informed of any status updates to the case.

d) All of the above.

Question 28

Which of the following assumptions / actions would be useful for a private investigator to make / take during the course of each investigation?

a) Assuming most investigations will not lead to a trial.

b) Administrative and procedural requirements should be handled with the utmost care.

c) Determining which clients are required to attend as witnesses when there is a criminal case.

d) All of the above.

Question 29

Which of the following statements is true?

a) Criminal convictions require a burden of proof beyond a shadow of a doubt.

b) In Civil matters, plaintiffs must prove the defendant is guilty beyond a reasonable doubt.

c) If found not guilty in a criminal matter, an accused will always win a civil lawsuit as a defendant on the same charge.

d) None of the above.

Question 30

Which of the following statements is true?

a) Criminal convictions require a burden of proof beyond a shadow of a doubt.

b) In Civil matters, plaintiffs must prove the defendant is guilty beyond a reasonable doubt.

c) If found not guilty in a criminal matter, an accused may still lose a civil suit as a defendant on the same charge.

d) None of the above.

Question 31

If a defendant lost in a Provincial Court and wanted to appeal the decision, which court would they have to attend next?

a) Provincial / Territorial Superior Courts

b) Court Martial Appeal Court

c) Provincial Courts of Appeal

d) Supreme Court of Canada

Question 32

Which of the following are not elements of the offence Intimidation (Section 423 of the Criminal Code)?

a) Persuades an individual to a particular action.

b) Uses violence of threats of violence to that person.

c) Persistently follows that person.

d) All of the above.

Question 33

Which of the following are elements in the offence Kidnapping (Section 279 of the Criminal Code)?

a) To confine or imprison a person against their will.

b) To transport a person out of Canada against their will.

c) To hold a person for ransom against their will.

d) All of the above.

Question 34

Which of the following actions could be considered an offence of Theft under section 322 of the Criminal Code?

a) An individual takes a loan out with his girlfriend's vehicle as collateral without her consent or knowledge.

b) An individual opens a security window and places a computer close by which he intends to take later.

c) An individual transfers money electronically from her boyfriend's bank account without his permission or knowledge.

d) All of the above.

Question 35

What is false pretence according to section 361 of the Criminal Code of Canada?

a) A false representation or statement, which is known to be false made with an intent to fraudulently induce the person to act on it.

b) A false statement, representation or action which causes a person to act in a manner or perform a task they would not normally be interested in doing.

c) A statement or representation which is not entirely accurate which causes an individual to perform or act in a manner they would not normally be willing to do.

d) A false statement or representation made by an individual which causes another person to act in a manner or perform a task they would normally not do.

Question 36

Which of the following would be considered aggravating circumstances in an offence of Fraud (Section 380 of the Criminal Code)?

a) An individual planned the fraud for several years and the crime too place over several years.

b) A ponzi scheme where hundreds of investors were victims which cost them collectively millions of dollars.

c) The offender was a politician who used his position in the community to help perpetuate the fraud.

d) All of the above.

Question 37

What are the six core steps for containing evidence?

a) Collect, manage, preserve, prioritize, personalize and record.

b) Collect, secure, preserve, identify, ensure continuity and log.

c) Collect, manage, preserve, identify, personalize and record.

d) Manage, secure, evaluate, identify, ensure continuity and discard.

Question 38

Which of the following is true regarding basic locator techniques?

a) They are the basis for all investigations.

b) They require minimal amounts of information and very little analysis.

c) There is very little concern to the individual being investigated and the general public.

d) All of the above.

Question 39

When attempting to locate an individual who has gone missing or an individual in order to serve legal documents, which of the following steps should not be taken without lawful authority?

a) Check public databases and Internet sources.

b) Advertisements in local newspapers requesting assistance.

c) Check with neighbours, known friends and associates for further information.

d) Obtaining bank, credit and income tax records.

Question 40

What information may be found at libraries that would prove useful to an investigation?

a) Publications, directories, government records and yearbooks?

b) Old newspaper stories, foreign government records, and notices of bankruptcy.

c) Business indexes, telephone books, old newspapers, memorials and probate notices.

d) Government records, phone books, old newspapers and notices of bankruptcy.

Question 41

Which of the following statements is true?

a) Private investigators are permitted to break minor laws in the Highway Traffic Act while conducting surveillance.

b) Private investigators should avoid contact with individuals represented by a lawyer.

c) Private investigators have authority to access personal banking records if conducing an investigation.

d) Surveillance may not be conducted to prevent the commission of an act.

Question 42

What is a common reason why private investigators may perform surveillance in teams?

a) Lack of trust from the client.

b) Multiple exit points from a target's location.

c) Additional revenue and profit for the agency.

d) All of the above.

Question 43

Which of the following aspects are important regarding the taking of statements from witnesses of an event?

a) To collect evidence only supporting the goals of your investigation.

b) To ensure there is an accurate record of the recollection of an event.

c) To trap a person into only being able to testify about what is specifically written in the statement.

d) All of the above.

Question 44

Which of the following statements is true?

a) It is best not to interrupt an individual during an interview.

b) You can correct mistakes on a witness statement without the knowledge of the witness if necessary.

c) The courts would prefer to have a witness statement that is grammatically correct as opposed to in the witness's own words.

d) All of the above.

Question 45

Why would private investigators be required to write reports and be familiar with standard protocols?

a) They may be used as evidence during criminal or civil trials.

b) They may be required for auditing purposes to ensure relevant work was performed for a client.

c) They may be used as managers and co-workers to continue work on investigations.

d) All of the above.

Question 46

Which of the following actions should generally be taken prior to attempting an undercover operation?

a) Interviewing all witnesses available.

b) Performing surveillance on key people involved in the situation.

c) Installing cameras to rectify a problem.

d) All of the above.

Question 47

Which of the following statements are false?

a) Typically it is the client's responsibility to determine if the police need to be informed regarding an investigation.

b) Actions taken regarding misuse of email will be dependent on whether an employee is using a company computer or a personal one.

c) Only a licenced private investigator is allowed to serve court documents.

d) All of the above.

Question 48

Which of the following statements is true regarding serving a notice under the Rules of Civil Procedure?

a) If a client does not sign acceptance, then service has not officially occurred.

b) It is improper to ask co-workers the whereabouts of an individual if they are deliberately trying to avoid being served.

c) If a person is refusing to answer the door, it is best to contact the client regarding steps to take to serve the individual.

d) The Trespass to Property Act does not apply to an individual attempting to serve a court document.

Question 49

What is the definition of prejudice?

a) Preconceived opinion not based on reason or experience

b) A widely held but fixed and oversimplified image or idea of a particular type of person or thing: "sexual and racial stereotypes".

c) A belief that one race is superior to another.

d) All of the above.

Question 50

Which of the following skills and concepts should private investigators know how to apply?

a) Understanding which groups of people tend to be more honest / trustworthy.

b) Make decisions based on hunches and strong gut feelings.

c) Making sound and defensible decisions supported by facts and research

d) All of the above.

Question 51

Which of the following would not be important mediums for communication on a daily basis for a private investigator?

a) Written reports.

b) Phone interviews and discussions.

c) Television interviews and advertisements.

d) Email and regular mail.

Question 52

Which of the following statements is true?

a) Private investigators must include opinion throughout any reports that they write for the clients.

b) Written reports are the only acceptable reports clients can be billed for.

c) Appropriate language should be used when writing reports for clients.

d) All of the above.

Question 53

Which of the following are general rules applicable to effective communication?

a) Be brief and concise.

b) Be clear and antagonistic if you have to be.

c) Exaggerate important details and be colourful with your language.

d) None of the above.

Question 54

Which of the following statements is true?

a) You should always use a polite, soft and respectful tone in all situations as a private investigator.

b) There are times when private investigators will have to be assertive.

c) Private investigators should have a goal to be confrontational with aggressive people first.

d) None of the above.

Question 55

Which of the following would be a verbal cue when communicating?

a) The volume and cadence at which the speaker is talking.

b) Hand gestures and movements used when speaking.

c) Facial expressions.

d) Body positioning.

Question 56

Which of the following statements is true?

a) Private investigators only need to work on their own and should focus on individual skills.

b) Private investigators do not need to be concerned about being exposed to high levels of stress.

c) Time management is a priority for private investigators as they often work on multiple projects.

d) None of the above.

Question 57

Which of the following statements accurately describes work situations common to a career as a private investigator?

a) Sitting stationary for long periods at a time.

b) Working in confined environments such as stairwells.

c) Performing monotonous / boring background research on individuals.

d) All of the above.

Question 58

Which of the following statements inaccurately describes work situations common to a career as a private investigator?

a) Sitting stationary for long periods at a time.

b) Routine days where you know exactly what to expect.

c) Performing monotonous / boring background research on individuals.

d) All of the above.

Question 59

Which of the following would be an important skill for a private investigator to posses?

a) They should be task focused and only work on one project until its completion.

b) They should be group focused and only work in teams.

c) They should be able to manage working on their own and at times in isolation.

d) All of the above.

Question 60

Which of the following is a situation, which is most easily completed independently?

a) A background check into a person applying to a key role in a private company.

b) An investigation of internal theft and corruption involving multiple potential suspects.

c) Surveillance of a suspect who lives in a large building with multiple exits.

d) A major investigation where many statements have to be taken from people in multiple jurisdictions.

1) D	16) D	31) A	46) D
2) A	17) A	32) A	47) C
3) D	18) C	33) D	48) C
4) A	19) C	34) D	49) A
5) C	20) A	35) A	50) C
6) D	21) D	36) D	51) C
7) C	22) C	37) B	52) C
8) A	23) B	38) A	53) A
9) D	24) D	39) D	54) B
10) C	25) B	40) C	55) A
11) C	26) A	41) B	56) C
12) C	27) D	42) B	57) D
13) C	28) B	43) B	58) B
14) B	29) D	44) A	59) C
15) A	30) C	45) D	60) A

Question 1

The PSISA was proclaimed into force on August 23, 2007.

Question 2

The Training and Testing Regulation made under the PSISA came into force on April 15, 2010. All private investigators must fulfill the mandatory requirements of the Training and Testing Regulation in order to be eligible to apply for a licence.

Question 3

Individuals are required to have a private investigator licence if they perform work, for remuneration, that consists primarily of conducting investigations to provide information on the character, actions, business, occupation, or whereabouts of a person.

Question 4

In order to be eligible for a private investigator licence, all individuals must:
- Have completed the required training and testing.
- Be at least 18 years old.
- Possess a clean criminal record, according to the Clean Criminal Record Regulation (note: not all criminal charges or convictions will prevent a person from obtaining a private investigator licence.)
- Be legally entitled to work in Canada.

Question 5

Private investigators are prohibited from holding themselves out as police officers, or performing police-related duties. For this reason, they are also prohibited from using the following words when referring to their work as private investigators:

- Detective or Private Detective.   - Law Enforcement.
- Police.   - Officer.

Question 6

Major offences such as aggravated assault will prevent a person from applying to become a private investigator as well as crimes which confirm dishonesty.

Question 7

Individuals found guilty of an offence under the PSISA could face a fine of up to $25,000, imprisonment for up to one year, or both. As such, it is crucial that private investigators comply with all aspects of the PSISA and its regulations to avoid the possibility of being named in a complaint or facing charges.

Question 8

Personal Information Protection and Electronic Documents Act (PIPEDA) is a federal statute, which sets out rules that govern the collection, use and disclosure of personal information by organizations engaged in commercial activities. A licensed business entity engaging in an activity regulated by the PSISA is likely subject to PIPEDA.

Question 9

There are circumstances in which consent is not required for the collection, use and disclosure of personal information such as publicly available records, including some judicial records, which are not subject to the restrictions on the collection, use and disclosure of personal information, as set out in the Act.

Also, according to Regulation SOR/2001-6, licensed business entities may receive or disclose personal information without the knowledge or consent of the individual to whom it belongs for the purpose of investigating the breach of an agreement or the contravention of a law if they are a corporation or other body:
(i) that is licensed by a province to engage in the business of providing private investigators or detectives and that has a privacy code that is compliant with the Canadian Standards Association Standard CAN/CSA-Q830-96, Model Code for the Protection of Personal Information, as amended from time to time; and,
(ii) that is a member in good standing of a professional association that represents the interests of private investigators or detectives and that has such a code.

Question 10

Private investigators should know about filing access requests for records that are subject to the above-noted Acts. Also, private investigators working for institutions that are subject to FIPPA or MFIPPA may be governed by one of these Acts, and may be limited in terms of what personal information they can collect, use or disclose.

Question 11

Private investigators may be required to observe a subject's daily activities, and should therefore be careful not to break any privacy laws. Anyone who is in a public place does not have a reasonable expectation of privacy, and their actions may be photographed or documented on video. However, a person in their home has a reasonable expectation of privacy and an investigator should not go onto their property in order to peer into their windows to observe them. In this situation, the best practice would be to observe the subject from the street, or other public property or thoroughfare. On the other hand, privacy becomes more of an issue if the subject is in their bathroom, for example, as opposed to their living room. Private investigators should exercise their judgment to determine when privacy becomes an issue, such as when the subject is at a gravesite, or participating in a religious observance, or when minors may be present.

Question 12

When videotaping, an investigator must remember that the integrity of the tape is paramount for court purposes; the original should not be altered in any way. There are restrictions in the Criminal Code about recording private conversations (see section 184 of the Criminal Code), so the best practice is to record without audio.

Question 13

Section 184 (1) does not apply when: a person who has the consent to intercept, express or implied, of the originator of the private communication or of the person intended by the originator thereof to receive it.

Question 14

Privacy concerns can also arise as a result of GPS tracking - GPS devices should only be placed on a vehicle to track its location with the permission of the owner of the vehicle. For example, if an employee is driving a company vehicle and the client is the owner of that company, the client may give written permission to the investigator to place a GPS device on the vehicle.

Question 15

Circumstantial Evidence is evidence from which a fact can be inferred, but doesn't stem from something that was witnessed directly. For example, the evidence of a witness who saw the accused stab the victim is direct evidence, while evidence that the accused owns the same kind of knife as the one used in the stabbing, the same type of gloves as the ones found beside the victim, and was seen in the vicinity shortly before the stabbing, is circumstantial evidence.

Question 16

Documentary evidence is traditionally defined as "any written thing capable of being made evidence no matter on what material it may be inscribed". This may include documents, books, cards, photographs, sound recordings, films, videotapes, microfiche, computer records, and other information recorded or stored by means of any device.

Question 17

Real (physical) evidence refers to things presented to a court. Real evidence can include material objects, such as a weapon or item of clothing, and demonstrations or experiments conducted for the benefit of the court.

Question 18

Unlike evidence involving the personal knowledge of a witness or particular facts, opinion evidence is evidence of what a witness thinks, believes or infers regarding the facts in dispute. The opinion must be based on facts that have been received into evidence. The opinion should come from an expert witness who can provide an educated/professional opinion on the evidence being presented. A judge would rule on whether the individual presenting an opinion would be considered an expert.

Question 19

According to subsection 2(1) of the Trespass to Property Act, a person may be found guilty of a trespass offence if:

They enter a location where entry is prohibited.
They engage in an activity that is forbidden on the premises.
They refuse to leave when asked to do so by the occupier or an authorized person.

If entry is prohibited or restricted, notice must be given to the individual, either verbally, in writing, or with the aid of signs or markings. Persons in violation of section 2 of the Act may be arrested without a warrant. A person who arrests someone under the authority of the Trespass to Property Act must contact the police as soon as possible and deliver the individual to a police officer.

Question 20

Private investigators have neither police nor peace officer powers. They have the same powers as any member of the public under the Criminal Code. Specifically, section 494 of the Criminal Code describes when it is appropriate for a member of the public to make an arrest. There are also provincial laws such as the Trespass to Property Act, which authorize private citizens to make arrests.

Question 21 / 22

Any person can make a citizen's arrest without warrant if they witness an indictable offence being committed. As such, private investigators should have an understanding of the distinction between an indictable offence and a summary offence. Typically, indictable offences are more serious; a lot of the offences that private investigators normally encounter are indictable.

Question 23

Once an arrest has been performed, the private investigator must deliver the individual to a peace officer as soon as possible. Where a private investigator is required or authorized by law to do anything in the administration or enforcement of the law, section 25 of the Criminal Code is applicable. In these circumstances, section 25 allows a private investigator (like all members of the public) to use as much force as is necessary as long as they act on reasonable grounds. However, section 26 states that individuals who use force are also criminally responsible for any excess of force in these circumstances.

Question 24

Section 25 of the Criminal Code allows a private investigator (like all members of the public) to use as much force as is necessary as long as they act on reasonable grounds. However, section 26 states that individuals who use force are also criminally responsible for any excess of force in these circumstances. The term "as much force as necessary" is generally regarded as no more than necessary. If you are able to arrest someone with very little contact or force, that should be the level you use.

Question 25

Section 27 of the Criminal Code authorizes individuals to use as much force as necessary to prevent the commission of an offence for which the perpetrator could be arrested without a warrant, and which could cause serious injury to a person or damage to property.

Question 26

Private investigators should have the skills and knowledge required to present evidence in a judicial environment. Private investigators may be required to prepare for legal proceedings, present evidence and follow up on the outcomes. Every investigation should be conducted as if the case could potentially go to trial and procedural and administrative requirements should be completed with the utmost care.

Question 27 / 28

Private investigators should have the skills and knowledge required to present evidence in a judicial environment. Private investigators may be required to prepare for legal proceedings, present evidence and follow up on the outcomes. Every investigation should be conducted as if the case could potentially go to trial and procedural and administrative requirements should be completed with the utmost care. It is always a good idea to keep key witnesses up to date regarding legal proceedings where they may be required.

Question 29 / 30

During a criminal trial, the Crown Attorney would need to prove beyond a reasonable doubt that the accused has committed the offence.

On the other hand, the burden of proof in a civil matter is less than in a criminal matter. In such situations, the obligation is for the plaintiff to prove the accused is guilty on the balance of probabilities.

Question 31

Matters do not go directly to the Supreme Court of Canada, and lower courts would have to hear and make rulings before this court would be considered.

Question 32

423. (1) Everyone is guilty of an indictable offence and liable to imprisonment for a term of not more than five years or is guilty of an offence punishable on summary conviction who, wrongfully and without lawful authority, for the purpose of compelling (not persuading) another person to abstain from doing anything that he or she has a lawful right to do, or to do anything that he or she has a lawful right to abstain from doing,

(a) uses violence or threats of violence to that person or his or her spouse or common-law partner or children, or injures his or her property;
(b) intimidates or attempts to intimidate that person or a relative of that person by threats that, in Canada or elsewhere, violence or other injury will be done to or punishment inflicted on him or her or a relative of his or hers, or that the property of any of them will be damaged;
(c) persistently follows that person;
(d) hides any tools, clothes or other property owned or used by that person, or deprives him or her of them or hinders him or her in the use of them;
(e) with one or more other persons, follows that person, in a disorderly manner, on a highway;
(f) besets or watches the place where that person resides, works, carries on business or happens to be; or
(g) blocks or obstructs a highway.

Question 33

Every person commits an offence who kidnaps a person with intent
(a) to cause the person to be confined or imprisoned against the person's will;
(b) to cause the person to be unlawfully sent or transported out of Canada against the person's will; or
(c) to hold the person for ransom or to service against the person's will.

Question 34

Every one commits theft who fraudulently and without colour of right takes, or fraudulently and without colour of right converts to his use or to the use of another person, anything, whether animate or inanimate, with intent
(a) to deprive, temporarily or absolutely, the owner of it, or a person who has a special property or interest in it, of the thing or of his property or interest in it;
(b) to pledge it or deposit it as security;
(c) to part with it under a condition with respect to its return that the person who parts with it may be unable to perform; or
(d) to deal with it in such a manner that it cannot be restored in the condition in which it was at the time it was taken or converted.
(2) A person commits theft when, with intent to steal anything, he moves it or causes it to move or to be moved, or begins to cause it to become movable.
(3) A taking or conversion of anything may be fraudulent notwithstanding that it is effected without secrecy or attempt at concealment.

Question 35

The key components of False Pretence are:

Known by the person to be false (can't be a mistake or simple exaggeration)
Intent to be fraudulent or deceitful to initiate an act. (statements or presentations have to be intended to induce an action.

361. (1) A false pretence is a representation of a matter of fact either present or past, made by words or otherwise, that is known by the person who makes it to be false and that is made with a fraudulent intent to induce the person to whom it is made to act on it.

Question 36

The following are all aggravating circumstances regarding the offence of Fraud:
(a) the magnitude, complexity, duration or degree of planning of the fraud committed was significant;
(b) the offence adversely affected, or had the potential to adversely affect, the stability of the Canadian economy or financial system or any financial market in Canada or investor confidence in such a financial market;
(c) the offence involved a large number of victims;
(c.1) the offence had a significant impact on the victims given their personal circumstances including their age, health and financial situation;
(d) in committing the offence, the offender took advantage of the high regard in which the offender was held in the community;
(e) the offender did not comply with a licensing requirement, or professional standard, that is normally applicable to the activity or conduct that forms the subject-matter of the offence; and
(f) the offender concealed or destroyed records related to the fraud or to the disbursement of the proceeds of the fraud.

Question 37

Private investigators may come across evidence that may be used in court, and should know how to collect and preserve evidence while preventing the evidence from becoming contaminated. They should also know how to present admissible evidence in court. The six core steps for containing evidence are collect, secure, preserve, identify, ensure continuity, and log.

Question 38

Basic locator techniques and pre-investigation are the basis for all investigations. For example, it would not be possible to conduct surveillance without knowledge of the subject's address.

This type of investigation has the potential to require an investigator to access and analyse a substantial amount of information. Therefore, it has the potential to pose the most concern to the individual being investigated and/or members of the general public. For this reason, basic locating and pre-investigative work should be conducted in the most thorough and responsible fashion possible.

Question 39

In cases where all previous address and contact information is no longer valid, it may be necessary to conduct an extensive background search. The investigator can make use of public databases and Internet sources in an attempt to locate the subject. Searches at the public library may also assist in confirmation of the outdated contact information and provide other resources to search. If none of these searches yields results, the investigator as a last resort may place an advertisement in the local newspaper with the last known address in hopes of finding the missing person or others that may have kept in touch with the person.

To keep the search as non-intrusive as possible, it is preferable for the investigator to avoid overt investigative techniques. Internet searches on the subject's address or employment record may offer insight in an insurance surveillance, but an investigator should not, without lawful authority, attempt to obtain documents such as credit records, income tax or bank records.

Question 40

Public libraries stock many useful publications and directories including telephone books, business indexes, trade magazines and yearbooks. Criss-cross directories of cross-referenced telephone numbers can also be found at a library, with telephone numbers listed in numerical order and associated with the subscriber's name. These sources of information can be particularly useful in cases where the available information is out-of-date. Newer information can be found through online databases that are updated more frequently.

Public libraries also have old newspaper stories, public notices and advertisements which may contain information on crimes and accidents, notices of bankruptcy, marriage, engagement and birth as well as obituaries, memorials and probate notices. Most libraries keep back issues of newspapers either on microfiche or CD-ROM.

Question 41

If the investigator is aware that the subject is represented by a lawyer, general practice is for the investigator to avoid having any verbal contact or interaction with the subject.

Question 42

Private investigators most commonly work alone on most surveillance cases, however in some cases two or more investigators may be assigned to work together. Reasons for this may include the subject's aggressive driving nature, multiple points of exit from a given location, or the subject's ability to run counter surveillance.

Question 43

The key purpose of taking a statement from a witness is to ensure an accurate record of the recollection of an event exists.

Question 44

Once the individual has started to talk, do not interrupt them. Take notes, but don't be too obvious. Control your emotions, and never react. Statements should be verbatim (word for word) transcription of the witness' recollection of the events.

Question 45

Private investigators regularly complete written reports of occurrences, duties performed and comprehensive descriptions of their tasks/observances. They need to create reports that are objective and standardized. They should be familiar with the different types of situational reports (e.g. legal or insurance) as well as basic report writing protocols such as: date, time, location, actions/behaviours, description of individuals, observations, time of completion, etc. In addition, they should be aware of the legal implications of reports (e.g. for auditing or evidence purposes).

Question 46

Generally the undercover operation is the last resort after all other investigative techniques have been exhausted or are not applicable. Other techniques may include assessments, interviews, interrogations, surveillance and camera installations.

Typically, private investigators will go undercover when they are required to investigate workplace-related issues. For example, a client may ask the investigator to pose as an employee in order to investigate possible theft being committed by another employee.

Question 47

Typically, it is the client's responsibility to determine if the police are to be informed.

According to established Canadian practice, the monitoring of employees' email without notification to the employee is acceptable if it is monitored on the company's server or network, as these are the company's properties. However, the practice may also be for employees to sign a release acknowledging that their computer activities may be monitored, whether the programs to do so are installed on the server or on individual computers that are connected to a company network.

If the investigator finds that an employee has been misusing a company computer, or using it to conduct illegal activities, the best way to protect the evidence is to isolate the unit and make sure no one else uses it.

On the other hand, if the employee is committing a violation through their personal/home computer (e.g. storing the company's intellectual property on a personal computer), it is best to simply have the client notify their counsel.

Generally speaking, any individual can serve documents. For this purpose, there is no requirement to be licensed as a private investigator. However, private investigators are often called upon by law firms, companies or individual citizens to assist with the service of documents. This may occur as part of an investigation where the intention is to locate the residence of individuals or subjects. Therefore, private investigators should be familiar with the Rules of Civil Procedure.

Question 48

A document must be served in the manner prescribed by the Rules of Civil Procedure. Unless an application for substituted service is completed, the document must be served personally upon the individual named where the rules require personal service. Service is affected once the person serving the document hands it to the person named, whether or not they actually accept the document. In a situation where the named party on the document refuses to open the door, the best action for the private investigator is to contact the client and advise of the situation. The lawyer or client will then make the necessary applications for substituted service.

It is crucial to identify clearly the person that is being served, both at the time of service and by affirming it in the Affidavit. Most often this is done verbally by having the person identify themselves by name. In some instances, such as when a Petition for Divorce must be served, the lawyer may request that the respondent provide a signature affirming the receipt of the documents. In this case, personal service is applicable and the private investigator must attempt to have the named party sign for the documents. In some instances, the investigator may need to have the named party show identification. The full instructions for such service of documents are often supplied directly by the client or their lawyer.

There are also times when a person may be uncooperative and try to avoid service. If this is the case, other methods for identifying the person may be utilized, such as asking coworkers, neighbours or other reliable sources that can be consulted to confirm the person's identity.

When a document is served, all applicable laws must be complied with. There is no justification for committing a criminal offence. For example, when serving a document to an individual in an apartment building where the investigator must gain access into the building, the investigator must comply with the Trespass to Property Act.

Question 49

Prejudice is a preconceived opinion not based on reason or experience. Answer B would be a stereotype and Answer C is a definition of racism.

Question 50

Skills and concepts that private investigators should know how to apply include:

- Recognizing differences between relevant/irrelevant facts and details
- Making sound and defensible decisions supported by facts and research
- Making appropriate judgments suited to the time-frame, risks and facts of the case and potential hazards/dangers in the situation.
- Prioritizing situations/decisions/tasks
- Drawing on legislation and laws to make decisions
- Preparing next logical steps required for a task/job
- Determining who should/should not have access to sensitive or confidential information/locations/people (PIPEDA)
- Recognizing ethical dilemmas.

Question 51

There are many different mediums for communication, including writing (reports, company policies), in-person, by phone, by email, through two-way radios, and by video recording.

Question 52

Private investigators must be able to communicate with a wide array of individuals both orally and in writing to obtain information. Information provided by a private investigator, presented orally or in writing, should always be clear and concise, and use appropriate language. Information should be conveyed accurately and without personal bias or opinion.

Question 53

Some general rules applicable to all communications are: be brief, be explicit, be concise, make sure you are understood and do not be antagonistic.

Question 54

It is important to adjust a communication style to accommodate a situation or an audience. Private investigators should be able to adjust their behaviour and demeanour accordingly. Communicating tactically, for example, ensures that private investigators can be assertive without being confrontational.

Question 55

In any situation, it is important to communicate in a clear and concise manner. The tone, volume, and cadence with which a message is presented can have a significant outcome in how it is received by its audience. Tone, volume, and cadence are especially important when dealing with people over the telephone where nonverbal cues are not available to help them interpret your reaction to the situation. Non-verbal cues have a very large impact on the comprehension of a conversation. Other non-verbal cues include body positioning (standing in an aggressive stance), hand movements, facial expressions (smiling vs. frowning), etc.

Question 56

Though private investigators may sometimes work in isolation, they must always interact with others, whether it is their employers, peers, clients, or the public. Being courteous and professional are always essential and help to establish rapports and build trusting relationships.

Private investigators can encounter high-stress situations and must maintain their professional composure. They should know how to properly react if exposed when conducting surveillance, how to control situations by asking questions, when one should identify oneself, and how to manage stress when dealing with isolation, driving and fatigue.

Private investigators may often work under stringent timelines, and should understand how to prioritize multiple tasks at once, and how to properly manage cases, time, different types of reports and dealing with shift work.

Question 57

Private investigators can encounter a multitude of situations and must adjust to changes quickly while maintaining their composure. They should know how to prepare for a variety of situations and how to adjust to work environments and demands (e.g. sitting for long periods, in stairwells, confined environments, etc.).

Question 58

Private investigators can encounter a multitude of situations and must adjust to changes quickly while maintaining their composure. They should know how to prepare for a variety of situations and how to adjust to work environments and demands (e.g. sitting for long periods, in stairwells, confined environments, etc.).

Question 59

Private investigators can encounter high-stress situations and must maintain their professional composure. Private investigators may often work under stringent timelines, and should understand how to prioritize multiple tasks at once, and how to properly manage cases, time, different types of reports and dealing with shift work. Private investigators may be assigned to situations where they need to work in isolation or within a team. They need to be able to work under a variety of circumstances and be able to understand the different working styles of colleagues (e.g. a two person surveillance, inter-agency cooperation).

Question 60

Private investigators may be assigned to situations where they need to work in isolation or within a team. They need to be able to work under a variety of circumstances and be able to understand the different working styles of colleagues (e.g. a two person surveillance, inter-agency cooperation).

GATB (General Aptitude Test Battery)

The General Aptitude Test Battery (GATB) is used for entrance exams for several security positions. You will have 7 minutes to answer as many questions as you can in the following topics:

- Math

- Problem Solving

- Spatial Folding

- Vocabulary

Scrap paper, pencils and erasers are allowed - no books, dictionaries, notes, writing paper, calculators, calculator watches or other aids are to be taken into the room. If you encounter a question you have difficulty with, take a guess and move on to the next one. Some agencies will disregard answers if there are too many random guesses (particularly at the end of the sections), so attempt to work through each question you can. Our math questions will be of the more difficult nature you will find on the exam. Be prepared to work through simple questions (6 + 9, 15 − 7, 8 x 9, 18 / 2, etc.) quickly.

Math

A B C D
1) ○ ○ ○ ○ ___
2) ○ ○ ○ ○ ___
3) ○ ○ ○ ○ ___
4) ○ ○ ○ ○ ___
5) ○ ○ ○ ○ ___
6) ○ ○ ○ ○ ___
7) ○ ○ ○ ○ ___
8) ○ ○ ○ ○ ___
9) ○ ○ ○ ○ ___
10) ○ ○ ○ ○ ___
11) ○ ○ ○ ○ ___
12) ○ ○ ○ ○ ___
13) ○ ○ ○ ○ ___
14) ○ ○ ○ ○ ___
15) ○ ○ ○ ○ ___
16) ○ ○ ○ ○ ___
17) ○ ○ ○ ○ ___
18) ○ ○ ○ ○ ___
19) ○ ○ ○ ○ ___
20) ○ ○ ○ ○ ___
21) ○ ○ ○ ○ ___

Total ___ / 21

Problem Solving

A B C D
1) ○ ○ ○ ○ ___
2) ○ ○ ○ ○ ___
3) ○ ○ ○ ○ ___
4) ○ ○ ○ ○ ___
5) ○ ○ ○ ○ ___
6) ○ ○ ○ ○ ___
7) ○ ○ ○ ○ ___
8) ○ ○ ○ ○ ___
9) ○ ○ ○ ○ ___
10) ○ ○ ○ ○ ___
11) ○ ○ ○ ○ ___
12) ○ ○ ○ ○ ___
13) ○ ○ ○ ○ ___
14) ○ ○ ○ ○ ___
15) ○ ○ ○ ○ ___
16) ○ ○ ○ ○ ___
17) ○ ○ ○ ○ ___
18) ○ ○ ○ ○ ___
19) ○ ○ ○ ○ ___
20) ○ ○ ○ ○ ___

___ / 20

Spatial Folding

A B C D
1) ○ ○ ○ ○ ___
2) ○ ○ ○ ○ ___
3) ○ ○ ○ ○ ___
4) ○ ○ ○ ○ ___
5) ○ ○ ○ ○ ___
6) ○ ○ ○ ○ ___
7) ○ ○ ○ ○ ___
8) ○ ○ ○ ○ ___
9) ○ ○ ○ ○ ___
10) ○ ○ ○ ○ ___
11) ○ ○ ○ ○ ___
12) ○ ○ ○ ○ ___
13) ○ ○ ○ ○ ___
14) ○ ○ ○ ○ ___
15) ○ ○ ○ ○ ___
16) ○ ○ ○ ○ ___
17) ○ ○ ○ ○ ___
18) ○ ○ ○ ○ ___
19) ○ ○ ○ ○ ___
20) ○ ○ ○ ○ ___
21) ○ ○ ○ ○ ___
22) ○ ○ ○ ○ ___
23) ○ ○ ○ ○ ___
24) ○ ○ ○ ○ ___
25) ○ ○ ○ ○ ___
26) ○ ○ ○ ○ ___
27) ○ ○ ○ ○ ___
28) ○ ○ ○ ○ ___
29) ○ ○ ○ ○ ___
30) ○ ○ ○ ○ ___
31) ○ ○ ○ ○ ___
32) ○ ○ ○ ○ ___
33) ○ ○ ○ ○ ___
34) ○ ○ ○ ○ ___
35) ○ ○ ○ ○ ___

___ / 35

Vocabulary

A B C D E F
1) ○ ○ ○ ○ ○ ○ ___
2) ○ ○ ○ ○ ○ ○ ___
3) ○ ○ ○ ○ ○ ○ ___
4) ○ ○ ○ ○ ○ ○ ___
5) ○ ○ ○ ○ ○ ○ ___
6) ○ ○ ○ ○ ○ ○ ___
7) ○ ○ ○ ○ ○ ○ ___
8) ○ ○ ○ ○ ○ ○ ___
9) ○ ○ ○ ○ ○ ○ ___
10) ○ ○ ○ ○ ○ ○ ___
11) ○ ○ ○ ○ ○ ○ ___
12) ○ ○ ○ ○ ○ ○ ___
13) ○ ○ ○ ○ ○ ○ ___
14) ○ ○ ○ ○ ○ ○ ___
15) ○ ○ ○ ○ ○ ○ ___
16) ○ ○ ○ ○ ○ ○ ___
17) ○ ○ ○ ○ ○ ○ ___
18) ○ ○ ○ ○ ○ ○ ___
19) ○ ○ ○ ○ ○ ○ ___
20) ○ ○ ○ ○ ○ ○ ___
21) ○ ○ ○ ○ ○ ○ ___
22) ○ ○ ○ ○ ○ ○ ___
23) ○ ○ ○ ○ ○ ○ ___
24) ○ ○ ○ ○ ○ ○ ___
25) ○ ○ ○ ○ ○ ○ ___

A B C D E F
26) ○ ○ ○ ○ ○ ○ ___
27) ○ ○ ○ ○ ○ ○ ___
28) ○ ○ ○ ○ ○ ○ ___
29) ○ ○ ○ ○ ○ ○ ___
30) ○ ○ ○ ○ ○ ○ ___
31) ○ ○ ○ ○ ○ ○ ___
32) ○ ○ ○ ○ ○ ○ ___
33) ○ ○ ○ ○ ○ ○ ___
34) ○ ○ ○ ○ ○ ○ ___
35) ○ ○ ○ ○ ○ ○ ___
36) ○ ○ ○ ○ ○ ○ ___
37) ○ ○ ○ ○ ○ ○ ___
38) ○ ○ ○ ○ ○ ○ ___
39) ○ ○ ○ ○ ○ ○ ___
40) ○ ○ ○ ○ ○ ○ ___
41) ○ ○ ○ ○ ○ ○ ___
42) ○ ○ ○ ○ ○ ○ ___
43) ○ ○ ○ ○ ○ ○ ___
44) ○ ○ ○ ○ ○ ○ ___
45) ○ ○ ○ ○ ○ ○ ___
46) ○ ○ ○ ○ ○ ○ ___
47) ○ ○ ○ ○ ○ ○ ___
48) ○ ○ ○ ○ ○ ○ ___
49) ○ ○ ○ ○ ○ ○ ___
50) ○ ○ ○ ○ ○ ○ ___

Total ___ / 50

Question 1
60026 + 99057 + 33282 + 80729 + 97468 =

a) 380562　　　　b) 370562　　c) 390562　　　　d) None of the above

Question 2
18546 + 15687 + 5217 + 47413 + 87001=

a) 173664　　　　b) 173864　　c) 173666　　　　d) None of the above

Question 3
85566 - 1206 =

a) 84330　　　　b) 85360　　c) 83360　　　　d) None of the above

Question 4
12943 - 7782 =

a) 5261　　　　b) 5161　　c) 6151　　　　d) None of the above

Question 5
95912 + 99806 + 91817 + 57611 + 37899 =

a) 383450　　　　b) 338450　　c) 353504　　　　d) None of the above

Question 6
78408 + 18163 + 38142 + 77104 + 86210 =

a) 298029　　　　b) 298027　　c) 289027　　　　d) None of the above

Question 7
62904 - 6549 =

a) 56555　　　　b) 56355　　c) 55355　　　　d) None of the above

Question 8
25978 - 7975 =

a) 17993　　　　b) 17893　　c) 18003　　　　d) None of the above

Question 9
805 x 30 =

a) 24250　　　　b) 22150　　c) 26150　　　　d) None of the above

Question 10
175 x 104 =

a) 18220　　　　b) 18200　　c) 18800　　　　d) None of the above

Question 11
4661 / 80 =

a) 58.26   b) 48   c) 55.29   d) None of the above

Question 12
4005 / 92 =

a) 43.53   b) 45.33   c) 47.2   d) None of the above

Question 13
511 x 111 =

a) 57721   b) 58721   c) 54721   d) None of the above

Question 14
195 x 46 =

a) 8870   b) 8970   c) 9870   d) None of the above

Question 15
8509 / 91 =

a) 92.6   b) 93.5   c) 94.1   d) None of the above

Question 16
5921 / 112 =

a) 54.87   b) 62.87   c) 50.87   d) None of the above

Question 17
100-25+37 =

a) 38   b) 110   c) 112   d) 88

Question 18
135 - 32 + 16 - 12 =

a) 107   b) 163   c) 195   d) 75

Question 19
(25+73) / (12+12.5) =

a) 2   b) 4   c) 6   d) 8

Question 20
{(12-8) + (15-2) - (3+2)} / (2+4) + (5+2) =

a) 9   b) 15/16   c) 7   d) 12/13

Question 21
(142-37) / (75-50) =

a) 5.7   b) 4.2   c) 3.4   d) 6.5

Question 1

A man drove for 5 hours. In that time he managed to complete 2/8 of his journey. How many more hours is he going to drive for?

a) 14　　　　　b) 15　　　　　c) 16　　　　　d) 17

Question 2

There are 18 pizza slices. Mike ate 1/2 of the pizza. Jim ate 2/6 of the pizza. Daren ate the left over slices. How many slices did Daren eat?

a) 8　　　　　b) 6　　　　　c) 4　　　　　d) 3

Question 3

Bill and Sue each had a collection of comic books. Bill told Sue, "If you give me 12 of your comic books, than I will have twice as many comics as you." Sue said the exact same statement. How many comics did each child have?

a) 30　　　　　b) 36　　　　　c) 42　　　　　d) 48

Question 4

What's my number? I am a three-digit number. My units digit is twice my hundreds digit. My tens digit is the sum of the other two. And I am the largest of such three-digit numbers.

a) 369　　　　　b) 246　　　　　c) 396　　　　　d) 264

Question 5

A number was divided by 7. When the answer was multiplied by 8 the result was 72. What was the number?

a) 63　　　　　b) 70　　　　　c) 54　　　　　d) none of these

Question 6

Twenty crates of computers weigh 1 tonne. If each crate weighs 10 kg when empty, how many kilograms of computers are there in one crate?

a) 20　　　　　b) 30　　　　　c) 40　　　　　d) none of these

Question 7

How many square millimetres are there in one square meter?

a) 100　　　　　b) 10 000　　　　　c) 1 000 000　　　　　d) none of these

Question 8

Shane can run at a rate of 5 m in half a second. How many meters can she run in ¾ of a minute?

a) 225 m　　　　　b) 450 m　　　　　c) 500 m　　　　　d) none of these

Question 9

A watch loses 5 seconds every hour. If it shows the correct time at 8 pm Monday, what time does it show at 6 am Wednesday?

a) 5:58:10 am   b) 5:57:50 am   c) 5:57:10 am   d) 5:56:50 am

Question 10

A stolen vehicle traveling at 60 km/h passes a stationary police vehicle with its engine running. The police car immediately starts out in pursuit and one minute later having covered a distance of half a kilometre, has reached a speed of 90 km/h and continues at this speed. How many more minutes will it take for the police to overtake the stolen vehicle?;

a) 1 minute

b) 1 minute 30 seconds

c) 2 minutes

d) 2 minutes 30 seconds

Question 11

Andrew, Ben and Chris form a business and share the profits in the ratio 6:3:2. If the net profit this year is $72 000, how much will Chris receive?

a) $22,500   b) $18,800   c) $13,090   d) none of these

Question 12

Jane ran for 20 minutes at 22 km/h. Then she walked for 10 minutes at 7 km/h and finished up with a light jog at 15 km/h for 30 minutes. How many kilometres did she cover in 60 minutes?

a) 22   b) 16   c) 20   d) 18

Question 13

Gurbir was loading up a pallet that could hold at most 150 kgs. He placed 3 balls weighting 15 kg each on the rack followed by 8 cases weighing 10 kgs each. What percentage of the rack's capacity has been reached?

a) 83%   b) 75%   c) 92%   d) 73%

Question 14

Water flows through a damn at a rate of 550 litres in 12 seconds. How much water will flow through in 3 seconds?

a) 120.3 litres   b) 137.5 litres   c) 142.6 litres   d) 183.3 litres

Question 15

George Bush has 72 statues in the White House. Each shelf holds 6 statues. How many shelves are needed to hold all the statues?

a) 7   b) 14   c) 9   d) 12

Question 16

Jane Green bought four tapes at $6 each. She then found $9 on the street corner. She now has $59. How much money did Jane have before he bought the tapes?

a) $90   b) $74   c) $63   d) $56

Question 17

$6844 + 23 + 82564 + 234 + 7423 =$

a) 97 088   b) 87 188   c) 95 088   d) none of these

Question 18

A singles dance had 75 people show up. If there were 5 more women than men, how many men are there?

a) 25   b) 30   c) 35   d) none of these

Question 19

How many kilograms in 180 pounds if there are 2.2 pounds to a kilogram?

a) 81.8 kg   b) 396 kg   c) 398 kg   d) none of these

Question 20

Shawna was given a 15% discount on a sweater that normally sold for $36.00. How much did she have to pay?

a) $5.40   b) $30.60   c) $32.55   d) none of these

Question 1

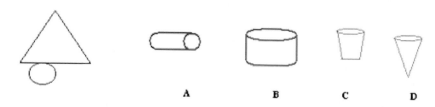

Question 2

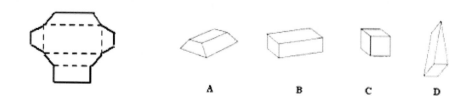

Question 3

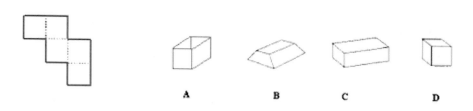

Question 4

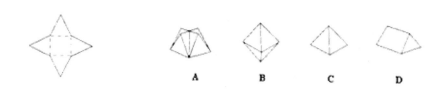

Question 5

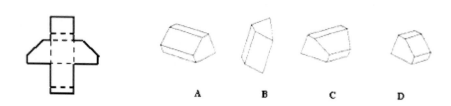

Question 6

A   B   C   D

Question 7

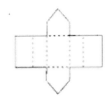

A   B   C   D

Question 8

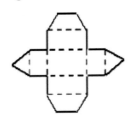

A   B   C   D

Question 9

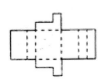

A   B   C   D

Question 10

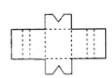

A   B   C   D

Question 11

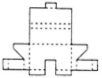

A   B   C   D

Question 12

A   B   C   D

Question 13

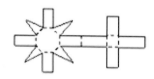

A   B   C   D

Question 14

A   B   C   D

Question 15

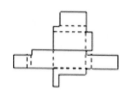

A   B   C   D

Question 16

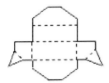

A   B   C   D

Question 17

A   B   C   D

Question 18

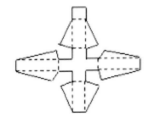

A   B   C   D

Question 19

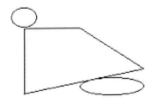   

A   B   C   D

Question 20

A   B   C   D

Question 21

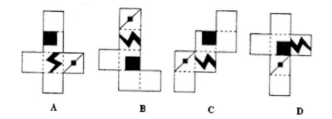

A   B   C   D

Question 22

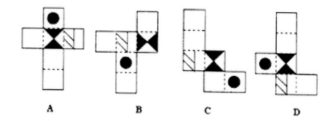

A   B   C   D

Question 23

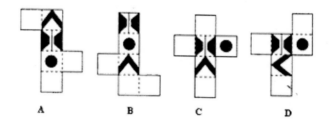

A   B   C   D

Question 24

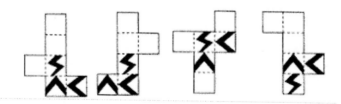

Question 25

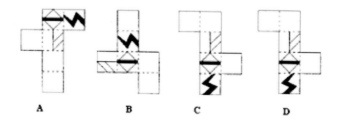

A   B   C   D

Question 26

 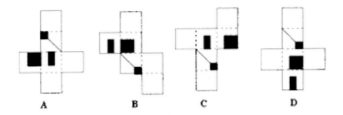

A   B   C   D

Question 27

 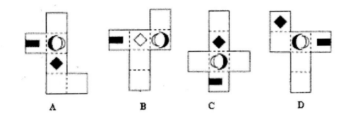

A   B   C   D

Question 28

 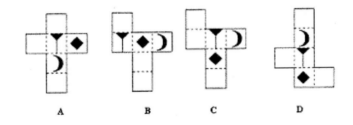

A   B   C   D

Question 29

 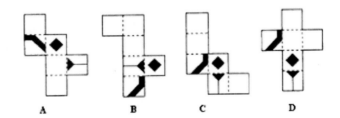

A   B   C   D

Question 30

 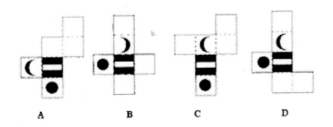

A   B   C   D

Question 31

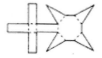

A   B   C   D

Question 32

A   B   C   D

Question 33

 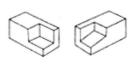

A   B   C   D

Question 34

A   B   C   D

Question 35

 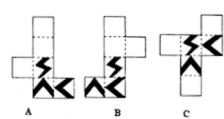 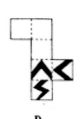

A   B   C   D

Question 1

Which two words have the same meaning?
a) usual
b) informative
c) routine
d) legal

a) a & b	b) a & c	c) a & d
d) b & c	e) b & d	f) c & d

Question 2

Which two words have the opposite meaning?
a) simple
b) lazy
c) diligent
d) careless

a) a & b	b) a & c	c) a & d
d) b & c	e) b & d	f) c & d

Question 3

Which two words have the same meaning?
a) extension
b) introduction
c) pretence
d) prologue

a) a & b	b) a & c	c) a & d
d) b & c	e) b & d	f) c & d

Question 4

Which two words have the opposite meaning?
a) candid
b) haughty
c) guarded
d) respectable

a) a & b	b) a & c	c) a & d
d) b & c	e) b & d	f) c & d

Question 5

Which two words have the same meaning?
a) worsen
b) manipulate
c) keep apart
d) manoeuvre

a) a & b   b) a & c   c) a & d
d) b & c   e) b & d   f) c & d

Question 6

Which two words have the opposite meaning?
a) impetuous
b) considered
c) studious
d) sacred

a) a & b   b) a & c   c) a & d
d) b & c   e) b & d   f) c & d

Question 7

Which two words have the same meaning?
a) hurl
b) jump
c) fling
d) pound

a) a & b   b) a & c   c) a & d
d) b & c   e) b & d   f) c & d

Question 8

Which two words have the opposite meaning?
a) anchor
b) join
c) listen
d) unfasten

a) a & b   b) a & c   c) a & d
d) b & c   e) b & d   f) c & d

Question 9

Which two words have the same meaning?
a) correct
b) release
c) ignore
d) rectify

a) a & b   b) a & c   c) a & d
d) b & c   e) b & d   f) c & d

Question 10

Which two words have the opposite meaning?
a) heinous
b) native
c) scenic
d) foreigner

a) a & b   b) a & c   c) a & d
d) b & c   e) b & d   f) c & d

Question 11

Which two words have the same meaning?
a) crazy
b) inane
c) difficult
d) foolish

a) a & b   b) a & c   c) a & d
d) b & c   e) b & d   f) c & d

Question 12

Which two words have the opposite meaning?
a) colourful
b) excellent
c) mediocre
d) indigenous

a) a & b   b) a & c   c) a & d
d) b & c   e) b & d   f) c & d

Question 13

Which two words have the same meaning?
a) disprove
b) dispel
c) disperse
d) scatter

a) a & b   b) a & c   c) a & d
d) b & c   e) b & d   f) c & d

Question 14

Which two words have the opposite meaning?
a) slow
b) unfair
c) explicit
d) unclear

a) a & b   b) a & c   c) a & d
d) b & c   e) b & d   f) c & d

Question 15

Which two words have the same meaning?
a) walk
b) shudder
c) shout
d) tremble

a) a & b   b) a & c   c) a & d
d) b & c   e) b & d   f) c & d

Question 16

Which two words have the opposite meaning?
a) nimble
b) calculate
c) confide
d) clumsy

a) a & b   b) a & c   c) a & d
d) b & c   e) b & d   f) c & d

Question 17

Which two words have the same meaning?
a) promote
b) jumble
c) dislodge
d) advance

a) a & b	b) a & c	c) a & d
d) b & c	e) b & d	f) c & d

Question 18

Which two words have the opposite meaning?
a) unkempt
b) touching
c) tidy
d) strong

a) a & b	b) a & c	c) a & d
d) b & c	e) b & d	f) c & d

Question 19

Which two words have the same meaning?
a) outcome
b) upshot
c) assurance
d) confuse

a) a & b	b) a & c	c) a & d
d) b & c	e) b & d	f) c & d

Question 20

Which two words have the opposite meaning?
a) slow
b) animated
c) shallow
d) lifeless

a) a & b	b) a & c	c) a & d
d) b & c	e) b & d	f) c & d

Question 21

Which two words have the same meaning?
a) broken
b) palatial
c) sad
d) magnificent

a) a & b
d) b & c
b) a & c
e) b & d
c) a & d
f) c & d

Question 22

Which two words have the opposite meaning?
a) tiny
b) colossal
c) reasonable
d) ruthless

a) a & b
d) b & c
b) a & c
e) b & d
c) a & d
f) c & d

Question 23

Which two words have the same meaning?
a) incarcerate
b) hate
c) imprison
d) emanate

a) a & b
d) b & c
b) a & c
e) b & d
c) a & d
f) c & d

Question 24

Which two words have the opposite meaning?
a) contrive
b) fluctuate
c) steady
d) inflate

a) a & b
d) b & c
b) a & c
e) b & d
c) a & d
f) c & d

Question 25

Which two words have the same meaning?
a) pedigree
b) ideal
c) grievance
d) complaint

a) a & b	b) a & c	c) a & d
d) b & c	e) b & d	f) c & d

Question 26

Which two words have the opposite meaning?
a) innocuous
b) inhibited
c) harmful
d) conventional

a) a & b	b) a & c	c) a & d
d) b & c	e) b & d	f) c & d

Question 27

Which two words have the same meaning?
a) forsake
b) nurture
c) shuffle
d) abandon

a) a & b	b) a & c	c) a & d
d) b & c	e) b & d	f) c & d

Question 28

Which two words have the opposite meaning?
a) hurdle
b) validate
c) cancel
d) finish

a) a & b	b) a & c	c) a & d
d) b & c	e) b & d	f) c & d

Question 29

Which two words have the same meaning?
a) ration
b) merge
c) gnarl
d) portion

a) a & b
d) b & c

b) a & c
e) b & d

c) a & d
f) c & d

Question 30

Which two words have the opposite meaning?
a) optimal
b) lethal
c) absurd
d) healthy

a) a & b
d) b & c

b) a & c
e) b & d

c) a & d
f) c & d

Question 31

Which two words have the same meaning?
a) ugly
b) huge
c) pertinent
d) gargantuan

a) a & b
d) b & c

b) a & c
e) b & d

c) a & d
f) c & d

Question 32

Which two words have the opposite meaning?
a) dabbled
b) justified
c) unwarranted
d) desecrated

a) a & b
d) b & c

b) a & c
e) b & d

c) a & d
f) c & d

Question 33

Which two words have the same meaning?
a) tremble
b) fawn
c) quiver
d) induct

a) a & b	b) a & c	c) a & d
d) b & c	e) b & d	f) c & d

Question 34

Which two words have the opposite meaning?
a) novice
b) expert
c) braggart
d) desperado

a) a & b	b) a & c	c) a & d
d) b & c	e) b & d	f) c & d

Question 35

Which two words have the same meaning?
a) retrieve
b) cringe
c) resell
d) recover

a) a & b	b) a & c	c) a & d
d) b & c	e) b & d	f) c & d

Question 36

Which two words have the opposite meaning?
a) wretched
b) happy
c) cumulative
d) incredulous

a) a & b	b) a & c	c) a & d
d) b & c	e) b & d	f) c & d

Question 37

Which two words have the same meaning?
a) muddle
b) study
c) confuse
d) clean

a) a & b   b) a & c   c) a & d
d) b & c   e) b & d   f) c & d

Question 38

Which two words have the opposite meaning?
a) flaccid
b) boring
c) firm
d) simple

a) a & b   b) a & c   c) a & d
d) b & c   e) b & d   f) c & d

Question 39

Which two words have the same meaning?
a) total
b) proliferate
c) foresight
d) vision

a) a & b   b) a & c   c) a & d
d) b & c   e) b & d   f) c & d

Question 40

Which two words have the opposite meaning?
a) dubious
b) scary
c) certain
d) serious

a) a & b   b) a & c   c) a & d
d) b & c   e) b & d   f) c & d

Question 41

Which two words have the same meaning?
a) enormity
b) colour
c) ambience
d) hugeness

a) a & b	b) a & c	c) a & d
d) b & c	e) b & d	f) c & d

Question 42

Which two words have the opposite meaning?
a) truncate
b) lengthen
c) exceed
d) annihilate

a) a & b	b) a & c	c) a & d
d) b & c	e) b & d	f) c & d

Question 43

Which two words have the same meaning?
a) nectar
b) decree
c) strength
d) ordinance

a) a & b	b) a & c	c) a & d
d) b & c	e) b & d	f) c & d

Question 44

Which two words have the opposite meaning?
a) unscathed
b) harmed
c) unborn
d) done

a) a & b	b) a & c	c) a & d
d) b & c	e) b & d	f) c & d

Question 45

Which two words have the same meaning?
a) boring
b) intrepid
c) tall
d) fearless

a) a & b	b) a & c	c) a & d
d) b & c	e) b & d	f) c & d

Question 46

Which two words have the opposite meaning?
a) candid
b) dejected
c) downcast
d) garish

a) a & b	b) a & c	c) a & d
d) b & c	e) b & d	f) c & d

Question 47

Which two words have the same meaning?
a) quick
b) demented
c) insane
d) handsome

a) a & b	b) a & c	c) a & d
d) b & c	e) b & d	f) c & d

Question 48

Which two words have the opposite meaning?
a) arrogance
b) stupidity
c) humility
d) happiness

a) a & b	b) a & c	c) a & d
d) b & c	e) b & d	f) c & d

Question 49

Which two words have the same meaning?
a) loyalty
b) thoughtfully
c) civility
d) allegiance

a) a & b	b) a & c	c) a & d
d) b & c	e) b & d	f) c & d

Question 50

Which two words have the opposite meaning?
a) shrink
b) decipher
c) grow
d) agree

a) a & b	b) a & c	c) a & d
d) b & c	e) b & d	f) c & d

Math	Problem Solving	Spatial Folding		Vocabulary	
1) B	1) B	1) D	21) D	1) B	26) B
2) B	2) D	2) A	22) D	2) F	27) C
3) D	3) B	3) A	23) C	3) E	28) D
4) B	4) C	4) C	24) A	4) B	29) C
5) D	5) A	5) D	25) A	5) E	30) E
6) B	6) C	6) C	26) C	6) A	31) E
7) B	7) C	7) D	27) D	7) B	32) D
8) C	8) B	8) A	28) A	8) E	33) B
9) D	9) C	9) A	29) D	9) C	34) A
10) B	10) A	10) B	30) B	10) E	35) C
11) A	11) C	11) B	31) C	11) C	36) A
12) A	12) B	12) B	32) D	12) D	37) B
13) D	13) A	13) B	33) A	13) F	38) B
14) B	14) B	14) C	34) D	14) F	39) F
15) B	15) D	15) D	35) A	15) E	40) B
16) D	16) B	16) B		16) C	41) C
17) C	17) A	17) B		17) C	42) A
18) A	18) C	18) A		18) B	43) E
19) B	19) A	19) B		19) A	44) A
20) A	20) B	20) B		20) E	45) E
21) B				21) E	46) B
				22) A	47) D
				23) B	48) B
				24) D	49) C
				25) F	50) B

Detailed Answer Key – Problem Solving GATB 1

Question 1

A man drove for 5 hours. In that time he managed to complete 2 / 8 of his journey. He many more hours is he going to drive for ?

Answer Key:

This answer is a multi step problem. The first step is to determine how long the ultimate journey will be. You will have to understand how fractions work for this problem.

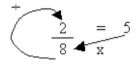

$\dfrac{2}{8} = 5$

The 5 hours completed represents 2 / 8 of the journey. To determine the entire trip you have to multiply the part of the trip completed to the denominator (bottom portion of the fraction).

5 x 8 = 40

40 ÷ 2 = 20

This number would then be divided by the numerator (top portion of the fraction). The result would be the total length of the trip (40 hours).

The second step would be to determine how much time is left. He has already driven for 5 hours. This becomes a simple subtraction problem.

20 hours total trip   20 - 5 = 15
   5 hours already driven

Question 2

There are 18 pizza slices. Mike ate 1 / 2 of the pizza. Jim ate 2 / 6 of the pizza. Daren ate the left over slices. How many slices did Daren eat?

Answer Key:

This question is a case involving multiplication, division, addition and subtraction. The first step is to determine how many slices Mike and Jim ate.

18 total slices   To determine the number of slices each guy
1 / 2 Mike   had, you must multiply the fraction by the
2 / 6 Jim   total number. This becomes a two stage
                        process.

$$18 \times \frac{1}{2} = \frac{18}{2} \qquad 18 \times \frac{2}{6} = \frac{36}{6}$$

Multiply the 18 by the numerator in both questions. The denominator remains the same.

$$\frac{18}{2} = 9 \qquad \frac{36}{6} = 6$$

After this is done you then divide the numerator by the denominator. Mike had 9 slices and Jim had 6 slices. By adding them together you find that 15 slices have been eaten. This now becomes a subtraction problem.

18 total slices   18 - 15 = 3
15 slices eaten

Question 3

Bill and Sue each had a collection of comic books. Bill told Sue, "If you give me 12 of your comic books, then I will have twice as many comics as you." Sue said the exact same statement. How many comics did each child have?

Answer Key

This will require a rather creative algebraic statement. Lets assume that "y" represents the number of comic books that both children have. If we increase "y" by 12, then it must equal twice the number of "y" - 12.

Here is how we right the equation:

$y + 12 = 2 (y - 12)$ The brackets have to be handled first. This is accomplished by multiplying 2 to both "y" and 12.

$y + 12 = 2y - 24$ Next we collect like terms, by subtracting "y" from both sides.

$12 = 2y - y - 24$ Followed by adding 24 to both sides.

$12 + 24 = 2y - y$ This can be calculated as:

$$36 = y$$

Because "y" represents the number of comic books that each child has, each child has 36 comic books.

Question 4

What's my number? I am a three-digit number. My units digit is twice my hundreds digit. My tens digit is the sum of the other two. And I am the largest of such three-digit numbers.

Answer Key

This question is very confusing when read. What it is actually saying is that there is a number which meets the following requirements.

A B C $c = 2 \times A$
             $b = A + C$
             Of all the possibilities, this is the largest.

The best way to attempt to solve this problem is to start of at the basics and calculate the easiest solution first, then increase the numbers till the largest number is reached to satisfy the third point.

A B C
1 4 3
2 6 4
3 9 6
4 12 8   Not Possible

Therefore the solution has to be 396.

Question 5

A number was divided by 7. When the answer was multiplied by 8 the result was 72. What was the number?

Answer Key

This problem requires you to work backwards through the information.

Step 1: The first step is to determine the value of the number after it had been divided by 7. This can be accomplished by dividing 72 by 8.

$72 / 8 = 9$

Step 2: Now we know that a number was divided by 7 which resulted in the value of 9. Therefore, if we multiply 9 and 7, we will solve the problem.

$9 \times 7 = 63$

Question 6

Twenty crates of computers weigh 1 tonne. If each crate weighs 10 kg when empty, how many kilograms of computers are there in one crate?

Answer Key

Step 1: The first step is to determine how much each crate weighs with the computers. This can be achieved by dividing the total weight (1 tonne) by the number of crates (20). You have to know that there are 1,000 kgs in a tonne.

$$
\begin{array}{r}
50 \\
20 \overline{)\,1\;0\;0\;0} \\
-\;1\;0\;0 \\
\hline
0\;0
\end{array}
$$

Therefore each crate with computers weighs 50 kg.

Step 2: Now it is a simple subtraction problem. Take the weight of each crate (10 kg) from the total weight of a crate and computer (50 kg).

$50 - 10 = 40 \text{ kg}$

Question 7

How many square millimeters are there in one square meter?

Answer Key

It is important to know your units of measurement.

1 metre   = 100 centimetres
        = 1000 millimetres

A square metre is achieved by multiplying 1 metre by 1 metre.
To determine the number of square millimetres in a square metre, you must multiply the equivalent number of millimetres together.

$$1000$$
$$\underline{x \quad\quad 1000}$$
$$1,0\ \ 0\ \ 0\ ,0\ \ 0\ \ 0 \quad \text{square milimetres.}$$

Question 8

Shane can run at a rate of 5 m in half a second. How many meters can she run in ¾ of a minute?

Answer Key

This problem is easy to solve if you understand the major fractions of time. 3/4 of a minute is equal to 45 seconds.

Step 1: Determine how fast Shane can run each second.

5 x 2 = 10 metres

Step 2: Multiply the speed she can run per second (10 metres) and the total number of seconds in 3/4 of a minute (45 seconds).

45 x 10 = 450 metres

Question 9

A watch loses 5 seconds every hour. If it shows the correct time at 8 pm Monday, what time does it show at 6 am Wednesday?

Answer Key

Step 1: First you have to determine how many hours have been used up so far. Remember each day is a 24 hour period.

6 am Wednesday to 6 am Tuesday =	24 hours
6 am Tuesday to 8 pm Monday =	10 hours
Total =	34 hours

Step 2: Calculate how many seconds have been lost during the total time.

34 x 5 = 170 seconds

This translates into 2 minutes and 50 seconds.

Step 3: Subtract the time lost from the new time on Wednesday.

```
  6 : 0   0 : 0   0     Remember that seconds and
      2 : 5   0         minutes only go up to 60.
  5 : 5   7 : 1   0 am
```

Question 10

The police car immediately starts out in pursuit and one minute later having covered a distance of half a kilometre, has reached a speed of 90 km/h and continues at this speed. How many minutes will it take for the police to overtake the stolen vehicle?

Answer Key

Step 1: First you must determine how far the stolen car has traveled in the first minute that it took the police car to reach 90 km/h. This is a very easy division question. Simply multiply the speed and time (remembering that 1 minute is 1/60 of an hour).

60 x 1/60 = 1 km   The stolen vehicle has traveled 1 km.

Step 2: Now that you know the police vehicle has traveled 0.5 km and the stolen vehicle has traveled 1 km. Now you must develop an algebraic equation to solve the problem.

	Police	**Stolen Car**
Speed:	90 km / 60 minutes	60 km / 60 minutes
Time:	y	y (has to be the same)
Distance:	0	+ 0.5 km

So the police traveling at 90 / 60 must travel equal the same time as the stolen vehicle travelling at 60 / 60 with a 0.5 km lead. This can be written:

(90/60) y = (60/60) y + 0.5   First collect the like terms. Subtract (60/60) y from both sides.

(90/60)y - (60/60)y = 0.5   Now you can subtract the two "y" variables (90/60)y - (60/60)y

(30/60)y = 0.5   Now you have to isolate the "y". Divide both sides by (30/60)

y = 0.5 (60/30)   Remember dividing by a fraction is the same thing as multiplying its reciprocal.

y = 30/30 or y = 1   It will take the police 1 minute to overtake the stolen vehicle.

Question 11

Andrew, Ben and Chris form a business and share the profits in the ratio 6:3:2. If the net profit this year is $72 000, how much will Chris receive?

Answer Key

This problem will require the use of fractions. If the ratio of the business is divided into lots of 6:3:2, then the entire business must be worth the sum of all parts (6 + 3 + 2 = 11). Chris should receive 2/11 of the total profit.

You therefore multiply 2/11 x $72,000.

$$\frac{2}{11} \text{ x } \$72,000 \quad = \quad \frac{\$144,000}{11} \quad = \quad \$13,091$$

Question 12

Jane ran for 20 minutes at 22 km / hour. Then she walked for 10 minutes at 7 km / hour and finished up with a light jog at 15 km / hour for 30 minutes. How many kilometres did she run?

Answer Key:

Problems like these require you to break the numbers down into their basic components. Remember that there are 60 minutes in each hour, so to solve this problem we must determine how far Jane ran during each part of the hour.

Step 1 requires that you solve how far she ran in the first 20 minutes. Because she was running at 22 km / hour and she ran for 20 / 60 of an hour, simply multiply the speed and the times together for a distance.

$$\frac{20}{60} \text{ x } 22 = 7 \text{ km}$$

Step 2: Perform this step with the other two distances as well.

$$\frac{10}{60} \text{ x } 7 = 1.2 \text{ km} \qquad \frac{30}{60} \text{ x } 15 = 8 \text{ km}$$

Step 3: Finally add up all three distances to determine a total distance run.

$$7 + 1.2 + 8 = 16.2 \text{ km}$$

Question 13

Gurbir was loading up a pallet that could hold at most 150 kgs. He placed 3 balls weighing 15 kgs each on the rack followed by 8 cases weighing 10 kgs each. What percentage of the rack's capacity has been reached?

Answer Key:

This is a two step problem that has to be solved by determining the total weight that has been placed on the pallet followed by determining what percentage of the capacity that weight represents.

Step 1 is to determine the total weight on the pallet. This is a simple multiplication and addition process.

3	x	15	=	45 kgs		45
balls		kgs			+	80
8	x	10	=	80 kgs		125
crates		kgs				

Step 2 is to determine the percentage this weight represents. This is accomplished by long division.

```
              0 . 8 3 3   =   83.3%
   150 | 1 2 5 . 0 0 0
       -  1 2 0 . 0
                5 0 0
            -   4 5 0
                  5 0 0
              -   4 5 0
                    5 0
```

Question 14

Water flows through a damn at a rate of 550 litres in 12 seconds. How much water will flow through in 3 seconds?

Answer Key

This will require the use of fractions. You can start by setting up an algebraic equation. In 12 seconds 550 litres will flow. You will have to assume that the same proportion of water sill flow. Therefore establish a relationship between the time and the water flow.

$$\frac{3}{12} = \frac{y}{550}$$

You should recognize that 3/12 can be rewritten as 1/4. This will make calculations easier.

$$\frac{1}{4} = \frac{y}{550}$$

Now you simply isolate "y" by multiplying both sides of the equation by 550.

$$\frac{550}{4} = y$$

550 / 4 = 137.5 litres

Question 15

George Bush has 72 statues in the White House. Each shelf holds 6 statues. How many shelves are needed to hold all the statues?

Answer Key:

This type of question is a straight division problem. You are asked to determine how many shelves holding 6 statues are required to hold 72 statues. Dividing 72 by 6 will solve the problem.

$$6\overline{)72}^{\,12}$$

Question 16

Jane Green bought 4 tapes at $6 each. She then found $9 on the corner and now has $59. How much money did Jane have before she bought the tapes?

Answer Key:

The approach you should use for this product is to work backwards. By doing this the problem can be solved with simple subtraction and multiplication.

$59   money now
$9   money found on corner
$24   money spent on tapes ($6 x 4 = $24)

Begin with the $59. You will have to subtract the $9 that she found, as Jane didn't have that before she bought the tapes.

$59 - $9 = $50

Finally you have to add back the money she spent on the tapes. This will give you the answer to the problem.

$50 + $24 = $74

Question 17

6844 + 23 + 82564 + 234 + 7423 =

Answer Key

If you have any problems answering this question, review the addition section of the teaching material. The main problem people have is failing to properly line up the numbers.

```
    6  8  4  4
          2  3
 8  2  5  6  4
       2  3  4
+  7  4  2  3
 9  7  0  8  8
```

Question 18

A singles dance had 75 people show up. If there were 5 more women than men, how many men are there?

Answer Key

This question will require an algebraic solution. You have "y" represent the number of men. Therefore the number of women can be represented by y + 5. When you add the women to the men, the total is 75. The equation is:

$y + y + 5 = 75$ You can group the "y's" together. $1y + 1y = 2y$

$2y + 5 = 75$ Now you have to isolate the "y". Begin by subtracting 5 from both sides of the equation.

$2y + 5 - 5 = 75 - 5$ or $2y = 70$

Next you will have to divide both sides by two.

$$\frac{2y}{2} = \frac{70}{2} \qquad \text{or} \qquad y = 35$$

There are therefore 35 men at the dance.

Question 19

How many kilograms in 180 pounds if there are 2.2 pounds to a kilogram?

Answer Key

This is a straight division problem. For every kilogram there are 2.2 pounds. All you have to do therefore is divide 180 / 2.2.

```
2 . 2 | 1  8  0              Remember to reposition the decimals
                             so that there is no decimal in the
          8  1 . 8           denominator (outside the bracket).
  22  | 1  8  0  0 . 0
    -   1  7  6
             4  0
          -  2  2
             1  8  0
          -  1  7  6
                   4
```

The solution is 81.8 kgs.

Question 20

Shawna was given a 15% discount on a sweater that normally sold for $36.00. How much did she have to pay?

Answer Key

This question can be solved with decimal multiplication. You should know that 15% can be written as 0.15 in decimals.

Step 1: Calculate the amount of the discount that Shawna will receive.

```
$   3 6 . 0 0
  x   0 . 1 5
$   5 . 4 0
```

Step 2: Now you simply subtract the discount from the regular price to determine how much money Shawna will have to pay.

```
$   3 6 . 0 0
  -   5 . 4 0
$   3 0 . 6 0
```